D0125380

Contents

Exchange Commission. Financial services conglomerates. The new specialty firms. New products explosion. Investment banking. Underwriting. Mergers and acquisitions. The exchanges and over-the-counter market systems (NASDAQ). Securities sales workers and brokers. Overall outlook for the securities industry.

Foreword

Money. These days none of us can live without it. It's the barter chip we trade to obtain the goods and services we use many times each day—at the grocery store, the dry cleaners, the gas station, the stationers, and the many other establishments we patronize for our personal and business needs. Most people go to work, get paid, and then use the money to maintain their lifestyles. This is the simplest, most basic use people make of money.

But, of course, there is much more we can and should do with our hard earned cash; things that are not so obvious and do not involve having to physically handle coins and bills. From this perspective, the use of money becomes more complex, and it enters a realm where "making your money work for you" is the goal at the end of the day. In this realm, the manipulation of money now occurs largely on paper and through the talents of people who are specially trained to do just that: "make your money work for you."

Opportunities in Financial Careers explores a range of jobs available to newcomers as well as those who are more seasoned in the world of finance. If you are just starting out and have little or no college education, you can read about the type of work a bank teller, clerk, or administrative assistant performs at the most well recognized of financial institutions—the bank. If you have decided to pursue a B.A. or M.A. in business administration or a C.P.A., you can read about what a commodities broker, investment banker, or public accountant needs to know to succeed in these jobs.

Whatever your particular interests are, the authors of *Opportunities in Financial Careers* break down the world of finance into its components: commercial banks, savings and loans, credit unions, mortgage associations, securities and commodities, insurance and real estate, financial services operations, corporate and industrial finance, and accounting. Within these broad categories a range of jobs is revealed. A small sample of the jobs you'll read about in this book include: bank examiner, manager of a bank branch, trust officer, loan officer, trader on the stock exchange, real estate agent, financial analyst, auditor, financial planner, and more.

For those who would like to be the one to "make money work," *Opportunities in Financial Careers* will start you on your way.

The Editors
VGM Career Books

1

INTRODUCTION TO
FINANCIAL CAREERS

*When a banker jumps out of the window, jump after him—that's
where the money is.*

—Robespierre

ACCORDING TO THE U.S. Department of Labor, financial institutions employed 7.3 million workers in 2001; it estimated that by 2003 the number would reach 7.9 million workers.

Financial institutions are defined in a number of ways:

- Depository institutions consist of banks, savings institutions, credit unions, and so forth, accounting for more than two million workers or 26 percent of all employed persons.
- Nondepository institutions include federal agencies, credit institutions, and so forth, employing about 730,000 persons.

- Securities and commodities brokers and dealers employ about 710,000 people. Although this group typically is not associated with financial intermediaries, it is extremely visible to the public. For example, the stock market is of daily concern to many people, and television and newspapers devote large amounts of coverage to its frequent fluctuations. One rarely witnesses such coverage of commercial banks, life insurance companies, or mortgage bankers.
- Insurance and real estate companies make up the final segment of financial institutions.

The securities group is the best paid, its workers making annual salaries of between 12 percent and 15 percent more than any other financial workers. According to the most recent statistics, those in securities management make approximately $102,910, compared to $74,000 for managers working in depository institutions. Even computer operators in securities are paid about $20,000 more than the equivalent job at depository institutions.

Among commercial banks the best paid are people working for foreign banks in the United States. The average annual wage of managers is approximately $100,020; computers operators earn about $66,100. The lowest salaries are paid to employees of credit unions, mortgage bankers, and real estate companies.

The greatest growth potential is in typical banking institutions, mainly commercial banks. This sector is quite stable, with a very low default rate even after periods of upheaval.

The securities market could be quite strong if one assumes a relatively good economic recovery. The life insurance business has also a strong potential. Residential real estate, though currently active, will most likely slow down by 2005. Commercial real estate, particularly for offices, is doing quite poorly, with sharp increases in vacancy rates.

In general, the financial institutions offer a great deal of stability and predictability as well as competitive salaries, and this will remain so in the foreseeable future.

How This Book Is Organized

According to the U.S. Department of Labor's Standard Industry Classifications (SIC), there are between 160 and 180 individual job categories within the financial institutions sector, which is made up of the following:

1. Depository institutions can be broken down into six major subcategories: central reserve, banks, savings institutions, credit unions, foreign banking in the United States, and functions related to banking.
2. Nondepository credit institutions consist of four entities: federal agencies, personal credit institutions, business credit institutions, and mortgage bankers.
3. Securities and commodities brokers, dealers, exchanges, and services are divided into four areas: securities brokers and dealers, commodities brokers, exchanges, and services allied with the exchange of securities.
4. Insurance carriers have seven subcategories: life, accident, and health; fire; marine and casualty; surety; title insurance; pension; welfare and others.
5. Insurance agents, brokers, and services make up another category.
6. Real estate has four categories: operators, agents and managers, title abstractors, and land subdividers.

Throughout this book you will find information and statistics on all these areas of the financial world to help you explore your career interest. You'll find other sources of information in the appendixes as well as a list of colleges and universities. There are hundreds of institutions offering majors in banking and finance; however, due to space considerations we could list only a small portion here. For a complete list, consult *The College Handbook*, published by The College Board. Most libraries have a copy. A good job in finance and banking requires a good, solid education.

Altogether financial institutions employ almost eight million people in areas as diverse as architecture, health care, food preparation, cleaning, construction, security, and transportation. However, the focus of this book is strictly on financial occupations, an area that employs about two million people.

Our main interests are with the first three job categories listed above. But even these categories contain too much—and, in many cases, irrelevant—information concerning our readers, as each major category can be further broken down into twenty-one job-related categories. Of these, only five are directly related to the finance and banking jobs described in this book.

The main category—business and financial occupations—encompasses twenty-two individual jobs in five categories and, according to the most recent statistics, employed more than 732,500 people. This is the category where most beginners in the field will find employment. Table 1.1 lists employment and salary statistics.

The next group—management occupations—employed almost 430,000 in about fourteen individual occupations including chief executives, sales managers, PR managers, computers managers, and so forth. Most jobs in this group are available to those who have already had some experience in business and finance occupations. Table 1.2 lists employment and salary statistics.

Table 1.1 Business and Financial Occupations

Institution	Employed	Mean Wage
Depository Institutions	288,580	$49,970
Nondepository Institutions	185,470	49,350
Securities and Commodities Dealers	136,900	69,740
Central Reserve	4,500	54,070
Mortgage Bankers	117,140	50,870
Total	732,590	54,800

Source: U.S. Department of Labor, Bureau of Labor Statistics: bls.gov

The next group—computers and mathematical occupations—encompasses about twelve categories including scientists, programmers, engineers, system analysts, statisticians, and so forth. This is a potential group for people who have computer skills. It also pays well. Table 1.3 lists employment and salary statistics.

Finally, office and administrative support occupations include about forty individual occupations such as bill collectors, bookkeepers, payroll personnel, tellers, file clerks, shipping clerks, computer operators, proofreaders, and so forth. This group is for beginners, and this is reflected in the lower annual salaries. Table 1.4 lists employment and salary statistics.

Table 1.2 Management Occupations

Institution	Employed	Mean Wage
Depository Institutions	226,350	$74,010
Nondepository Institutions	71,180	82,650
Securities and Commodities Dealers	92,900	102,910
Central Reserve	2,230	87,830
Mortgage Bankers	34,350	85,800
Total	427,010	86,640

Source: U.S. Department of Labor, Bureau of Labor Statistics: bls.gov

Table 1.3 Computers and Mathematical Occupations

Institution	Employed	Mean Wage
Depository Institutions	74,740	$57,630
Nondepository Institutions	25,250	57,750
Securities and Commodities Dealers	44,170	66,210
Central Reserve	3,270	61,330
Mortgage Bankers	7,510	54,830
Total	154,940	59,548

Source: U.S Department of Labor, Bureau of Labor Statistics: bls.gov

Life insurance and real estate occupations are covered in Chapter 8.

Comments Regarding Statistical Information

The definition of the financial sector described above that includes banks, savings and loans, credit unions, nondepository institutions, securities, holding and investment offices, insurance, and real estate comes from the Federal Reserve Board.

Most of the information included here comes from government sources such as the Federal Reserve Board, U.S. Department of Labor, Federal Deposit Insurance Corporation, Department of Treasury, U.S. Bureau of Economic Analysis, National Credit

Table 1.4 Office and Administrative Support Occupations

Institution	Employed	Mean Wage
Depository Institutions	1,330,620	$24,740
Nondepository Institutions	375,220	28,650
Securities and Commodities Dealers	269,220	33,530
Central Reserve	12,260	29,190
Mortgage Bankers	144,550	30,090
Total	2,131,870	29,240

Source: U.S. Department of Labor, Bureau of Labor Statistics: bls.gov

Union Administration, and the U.S. Federal Housing Finance Board, as well as from institutions representing various business entities such as realtors, home builders, insurance companies, and so on.

The Department of Labor has a long list of various occupations (twelve pages for commercial banks) with 123 individual occupations. A list of approximately ten occupations selected from the individual business and financial operations occupations for 1999 and 2001, with a percentage calculation of annual changes, is presented in each chapter.

Some data are currently available only for 2000 and 2001, and a few for 2002 and 2003. As far as the number of employees and establishments is concerned, most of the data come from the Standard Industrial Classification (SIC) information issued by the U.S. Department of Labor. Some data come from County Business Pattern data and some from the Federal Reserve Board. If you examine the data closely you may find some discrepancy between various databases. However, this should not be of major concern because differences will occur given the size and population of the country, the various ways data are collected, the purpose of collection, and the timing of collection. Most wage data are available only for 2001, but these figures will give you a good idea of what to expect.

Table 1.5 summarizes the occupations and salaries you can expect to find in banks, savings institutions, credit unions, and foreign banks in the United States. More detailed information is included throughout the rest of the book.

Financial Sector Remains Strong

Contrary to what you may read, the U.S. financial institutions sector remains stronger than ever. Its share of the U.S. economy grew

Table 1.5 U.S. Commercial Banks, Savings Institutions, Credit Unions, Foreign Banks, and Branches in Selected Business and Financial Occupations, Mean Annual Salaries

Occupation Title	Banks	Saving	Credit	Foreign
Loan Officers	$50,040	$44,590	$33,310	$89,030
Management Analysts	60,310	53,450	47,580	72,100
Accountants and Auditors	46,130	44,430	38,690	56,770
Budget Analysts	55,480	55,250	43,930	65,800
Credit Analysts	46,020	44,220	34,460	63,180
Financial Analysts	56,800	54,610	44,840	80,450
Personal Financial Advisors	63,740	57,770	42,010	85,250
Financial Examiners	50,800	48,920	40,120	NA
Loan Counselors	37,820	35,970	33,310	NA
Total	75,490	47,540	34,960	69,650

Source: U.S. Department of Labor, Bureau of Labor Statistics, SIC 602—Commercial Banks, bls.gov

in terms of assets, services provided, and people employed, and its share of the Gross National Product—the goods and services we collectively produce—increased from 17.4 percent in 1990 to 19.6 percent in 2000. This was an increase of nearly a trillion dollars. Its share of the GNP in the year of 2003 was estimated to exceed 20 percent and $2.075 trillion. However, as the past has demonstrated, the United States is not immune to recessions.

Another way to measure the expansion of the U.S. financial sector is to compare its net flow of funds. In 1980 the total flow was $14.1 trillion; in 2003 it reached $92 trillion.

Since 1950 the United States has averaged about 1 percent growth annually. In 1950 there were approximately 152.3 million U.S. residents. In 1980 this figure reached 226.5 million, and in 1990 it reached 248.7 million. According to the U.S. Bureau of the Census, the resident population of the United States, as of September 1, 2003, was 292.0 million, an increase of 43.3 million people in twelve years. This is ten million people more than the population of the state of California. Every eleven seconds we gain another person. All these people will require a great deal of financial services.

In the ten years between January 1993 and January 2003, the number of U.S. workers increased by about 1.7 million every year. As mentioned at the beginning of this chapter, financial careers provide employment for nearly eight million people, and, with very few exceptions, opportunities in these careers are expected to grow over the next decade. According to the Department of Labor, in 1999 there were just under 7.5 million people working in financial sectors, and by September 2003 this number had increased to 7.85 million, a jump of 330,000. The summary of total employment of the eight financial sectors shows that three sectors account for almost 69 percent of the total employment. These sectors are: depository institutions (27.9 percent), insurance carriers (21.0 percent), and real estate (20.0 percent).

Careers in the field of finance offer a variety of rewarding employment opportunities. Many of the careers require advanced degrees and advanced professional training, which eventually lead to managerial positions. Others require bachelor's degrees with a concentration in mathematics, statistics, or economics. Still others, particularly trainee positions, require a high school education or limited college experience.

Depository institutions such as commercial banks, savings institutions, and credit unions have come a long way from the days when employees were either tellers/bookkeepers or managers and loan officers. Today, people working for financial institutions need and use a variety of interrelated skills. Their work may involve being an economist, a teacher, or an agricultural expert, to name but a few of the many professions represented in today's economy. Much of what is required of depository institutions depends upon what type of lending or what types of services they provide for the community.

The growth of the U.S. population provides more potential for overall employment, particularly in the financial sector. Just about everything we do requires financing. Whether buying or selling stocks and bonds, saving for investments or retirement, buying a house, insuring against potential loss or liability, investing in business or in a new invention—all these require financial services. Because financial institutions are crossing lines regarding the financial services they offer, expertise in a wide variety of services is becoming commonplace and is often required for advancement.

As a part of the overall financial sector, the accounting profession is also expected to expand into the next century. Accountants provide the information necessary to determine and evaluate present and projected economic activities or individual projects that require financing. Professional accountants develop and apply their skills in fields as diverse as auditing, taxation, management policy, information systems, computer operations, and many others. Excluding insurance and real estate, there were 52,850 accountants, making between $46,000 and $55,500 a year, and 90,270 bookkeepers, making between $27,000 and $36,500 a year, working at financial institutions in 2001.

More and more, financial services are becoming a worldwide phenomenon, helped by a fantastic explosion of computer technology. It takes a few seconds to transfer funds from virtually anywhere in the world—a dream just ten years ago. You can buy securities in the blink of an eye. You can communicate your wishes by e-mail or fax from your home. To be on the cutting edge requires intensive training in communication technology and a constant update of education, even though interfaces are becoming more user-friendly to reach a broader audience.

The improving technology and worldwide competition coming from better-educated foreign workers with considerably lower wages are threatening the high-paying jobs of American white-collar workers. It's impossible to stop globalization. We must face the unprecedented competition from abroad and look for new opportunities. Our talented workforce will "redeploy their skills in new directions and endeavors," said John Challenger, chief executive of outsourcing firm Challenger, Gay, and Christmas, at the congressional hearings on June 18, 2003.

If you are looking for a career in which your energies and talents are most likely to be rewarded through monetary compensation, prestige, challenge, and recognition, you will want to take a closer look at some of the great variety of careers available in the field of finance. In addition to the U.S. Department of Labor, a good source of employment data is the website salary.com. It tracks employment trends across the nation.

2

U.S. Banking History and Regulations

Though banking has existed in some form for several centuries, it was sometime in the early seventeenth century that modern banking is said to have had its start. The word *bank* comes from the Italian word *banca* ("bench"), where Italian bankers conducted their business on the open streets.

Later in history, English traders and merchants began storing precious metals like gold and silver in the vaults of goldsmiths. The goldsmiths would issue paper receipts or notes for the gold and silver, because the notes were much easier to carry around. People then began using the paper notes, instead of the precious metals, as money. The goldsmiths, meanwhile, began to lend out the gold and silver for a fee. Some of them began paying interest to attract new deposits of gold and silver.

In the United States the first bank, the Bank of North America, was established in 1781 in Philadelphia. Ten years later, the U.S.

Congress chartered the first Bank of the United States but did not renew its charter in 1811. The second Bank of the United States was chartered in 1816 and closed in 1836.

In 1838 New York adopted the Free Banking Act. As a result, free banking spread rapidly to other states. In many western states it degenerated into "wildcat" banking. Bank notes were issued against little or no security, and credit was overextended, resulting in a depression with waves of bank failures. To correct such conditions, in 1863 Congress passed the National Bank Act, which provided for a system of banks to be chartered by the federal government.

Several banking panics caused by the expansion of credit, inadequate bank reserves, and inelastic currency prompted Congress in 1908 to create the National Monetary Commission to investigate the banking and currency fields and to recommend legislation. Its suggestions were embodied in the Federal Reserve Act (1913), and that provided for a central banking organization, the Federal Reserve System.

The Glass-Steagall Act of 1932 and the Banking Act of 1933 together formed an extensive reform measure designed to correct the abuses that had led to numerous bank crises in the years following the stock market crash of 1929. The Glass-Steagall Act prohibited commercial banks from involvement in the securities and insurance businesses. The Banking Act strengthened the powers of supervisory authorities, increased controls over the volume and use of credit, and provided for the insurance of bank deposits under the Federal Deposit Insurance Corporation (FDIC). The Banking Act of 1935 strengthened the powers of the Federal Reserve Board of Governors in the field of credit management, tightened existing restrictions on banks engaging in certain activities, and enlarged the supervisory powers of the FDIC.

The Function of Banking

In the United States, banks had two main functions as late as the Civil War: accepting deposits and making short-term loans to businesses—two functions that banks still fulfill today. A small bank usually needed only a few employees: a president and a cashier who ran the bank and made the loans, and a combination clerk/teller/bookkeeper who handled deposits and withdrawals and kept the bank's records.

Checking was introduced in the United States shortly before the Civil War but did not come into general use until about 1875. Most banking until that time was done on a cash basis. Other services were gradually added to banking's repertoire after checking became more popular. Real estate loans came into being around 1916 and personal and short-term loans in the 1930s. With each new service came the need for more and different kinds of employees to serve the requirements of the expanded bank.

Money is such a routine part of our lives that its existence is too often taken for granted. Because money is used as a tool to help facilitate transactions, it must be readily available. Today in the United States there are only two kinds of money in use in any significant amount—currency (paper money and coins) and demand deposits (checking accounts). The distribution of these two components depends solely upon the public's preferences. However, the actual supply of money is another matter.

The Riegle-Neal Interstate Banking and Branching Efficiency Act of 1994 allows for greater consolidation and branching within the banking industry. Bank holding companies can now acquire banks in any state, and interstate bank mergers are now permitted subject to certain requirements and Community Reinvestment Act evaluations.

Meanwhile, the liberalization of branch banking laws by several states is continuing. Some states have adopted statewide branching, while others introduced branching within the county or adjacent counties of a bank's main office. Even unit banking states—those restricting branching—are permitting some expansion of branching services in the form of electronic fund-transfer facilities or drive-ins.

Creation of the Federal Reserve System

The Federal Reserve System, also known as the Fed, is the central bank of the United States. It was created by Congress with the passage of the Federal Reserve Act in 1913. The Federal Reserve System is composed of a central, governmental agency—the Board of Governors—in Washington, D.C., and twelve regional Federal Reserve Banks located in major cities throughout the nation. The Federal Reserve System is not "owned" by anyone and is not a private, profit-making institution. Instead, it is an independent entity within the government, having both public purposes and private aspects.

As expressed by its founders, the original purposes of the Federal Reserve System were to give the country a flexible currency, to provide facilities for discounting commercial paper, and to improve the supervision of the nation's banks.

From the outset it was recognized that the original purposes of the Federal Reserve System were, in fact, the broader aspects of U.S. economic policy, such as economic stability, growth, and a high level of employment. The Federal Reserve Board contributes to these broad economic goals through its ability to influence the availability and cost of money and credit in the economy. As the nation's central bank, it attempts to ensure that the growth of money and credit is large enough to provide for a rising standard of living. In the short run, the Fed seeks to combat inflation; as a lender of last resort, it uses the various financial instruments available to it.

The Federal Reserve derives its authority from the U.S. Congress. It is considered an independent central bank because its decisions do not have to be ratified by the President or anyone else in the executive or legislative branch of government. It does not receive funding appropriated by Congress, and the terms of the members of the Board of Governors span multiple presidential and congressional terms. However, the Federal Reserve is subject to oversight by Congress, which periodically reviews its activities and can alter its responsibilities by statute. Also, the Federal Reserve must work within the framework of the overall objectives of economic and financial policy established by the government. Therefore, the Federal Reserve can be more accurately described as "independent within the government."

The Federal Open Market Committee (FOMC) is charged under the law with overseeing open market operations, the principal tool of national monetary policy. (Open market operations are the buying and selling of government securities.) The committee sets monetary policy by specifying the short-term objective for those operations, which is currently a target level for the federal funds rate (the rate that commercial banks charge on overnight loans among themselves). The FOMC also directs operations undertaken by the Federal Reserve in foreign exchange markets, although any intervention in foreign exchange markets is coordinated with the U.S. Treasury, which has responsibility for formulating U.S. policies regarding the exchange value of the dollar.

Stimulation of Economic Growth

The Federal Reserve Act specifies that the FOMC should seek "to promote effectively the goals of maximum employment, stable prices, and moderate long-term interest rates." At each meeting, the FOMC closely examines a number of indicators of current and prospective economic developments. Then, cognizant that its actions affect economic activity with a lag, it must decide whether to alter the federal funds rate. A decrease in the federal funds interest rate stimulates economic growth, but an excessively high level of economic activity can cause inflation pressures to build to a point that ultimately undermines the sustainability of an economic expansion. An increase in the federal funds interest rate will curb economic growth and help contain inflation pressures and thus can promote the sustainability of an economic expansion, but too large an increase could retard economic growth too much. The committee's actions on interest rates are undertaken to achieve the maximum rate of economic growth consistent with price stability and moderate long-term interest rates.

Board of Governors

The seven members of the Board of Governors of the Federal Reserve System are nominated by the President and confirmed by the Senate. A full term is fourteen years. One term begins every two years on even-numbered years on February 1. A member who serves a full term may not be reappointed. A member who completes an unexpired portion of a term may be reappointed. All terms end on their statutory date regardless of the date on which the member is sworn into office.

The Fed has also been entrusted with many supervisory and regulatory functions. Among these functions it has the responsibility for the amount of credit that may be used for purchasing securities; it establishes the maximum interest rates that member commercial banks may pay on savings and time deposits; and it supervises state-chartered banks and regulates the foreign activities of all U.S. banks. The Fed also has the responsibility for administering the laws that regulate bank holding companies. Additionally, it establishes the rules of disclosure about credit changes and repayment terms to which all lenders of consumer credit must adhere.

Central Banks' Independence

Most countries have central banks that perform duties similar to the Fed: the Bank of England was established at the end of the seventeenth century; the Bank of France was established by Napoleon in 1800; and the Bank of Canada began operations in 1935.

Central banks have varying degrees of independence within their governments, depending on the economic, political, and historical circumstances surrounding their establishment and their development.

It is often said that the Fed is an independent central bank. This is true in some respects. Decisions made by the Fed do not have to be ratified by the President or one of his appointees. However, the Fed must report to Congress on its policies. The President makes all appointments to the Board of Governors of the Fed—with the consent of the Senate. Furthermore, the President designates two members of the Board of Governors to be chairperson and vice chairperson. As the Fed carries out its responsibilities, its officials are in constant contact with other policymakers in the government.

As was previously mentioned, the Fed operates within the general framework of national goals. In the economic sphere, the Fed helps to achieve those goals by influencing the availability and cost of bank reserves, bank credit, and money. This is done through open market operations—purchases and sales of securities—and by varying reserve requirements. In addition, the Fed sets the discount rate, directly affecting the cost of reserves borrowed by member banks.

Changes in bank reserves, in turn, influence the ability of banks to expand loans and investments. For example, if the Fed adds to a member bank's monetary reserve, the bank will generally try to make new loans and investments. This tends to exert a downward pressure on interest rates. At the same time that banks are buying securities or making loans, they will be adding to the deposits of the public. The public's willingness to hold the deposits is, in turn, influenced by the prevailing level of short- and long-term interest rates.

The operations of the Federal Reserve System are conducted through a network of twelve Federal Reserve Banks located in Boston, New York, Philadelphia, Cleveland, Richmond, Atlanta, Chicago, St. Louis, Minneapolis, Kansas City, Dallas, and San Francisco. Branches of reserve banks have been established in twenty-four additional cities.

Each Reserve Bank is an incorporated institution with its own board of directors. These directors oversee the operations of their bank under the overall supervision of the Board of Governors. Subject to approval by the board, the directors establish the interest rates the bank charges on short-term collateral loans to member banks and on any loans that may be extended to nonmember institutions.

Impact of the Fed's Moves Needs to Be Watched Carefully

What the Fed does affects everybody here and overseas. When considering a new employment opportunity, it is always prudent to examine the Fed's monthly statement concerning the economy and any action it took. For instance, in the statement made on May 7, 2003, the Fed said that it was prepared to cut interest rates again partly out of concern that any further substantial drop in inflation would pose a danger for economic recovery. If you are looking for employment in the financial sector, the assurance that the Fed will not raise interest rates means that it is more concerned with recovery and less with inflation. This suggests that for the next two years it may be a good time to look for employment, as the Fed indicates its willingness to support the recovery.

As of mid-2003 we have had one of the lowest interest rates on record, as the Fed is trying to stimulate the sluggish economic growth and help employment.

The U.S. economy continued to improve in the third quarter of 2003 at an 8.2 percent annual rate of growth, the fastest rate since 1984 when the economy grew at a 9.0 percent annual rate, helped by tax cuts and low interest rates. The unemployment rate dropped to 5.9 percent, and consumption expenditures kept growing at a sturdy 6.6 percent annual rate. Consumer spending was strong, with a jump in real disposable income, reflected by the lower withholding tax rates. Corporate profits in the third quarter of 2003 were up almost 12 percent—30 percent from the third quarter of 2002.

In mid-December of 2003 the Federal Reserve Board stated: "The Federal Open Market Committee decided today to keep its target for the federal funds rate at 1 percent. The Committee continues to believe that an accommodative stance of monetary policy, coupled with robust underlying growth in productivity, is providing important ongoing support to economic activity. The evidence accumulated over the intermeeting period confirms that output is expanding briskly, and the labor market appears to be improving modestly. Increases in core consumer prices are muted and expected to remain low. With inflation quite low and resource use slack, the Committee believes that policy accommodation can be maintained for a considerable period."

The lowest rate set by the Fed was at 0.63 percent in May 1958. The second-lowest was at 0.83 percent in November 1954. The highest rate ever was at 19.08 percent in January 1981. The postwar period was characterized by rates below 3.0 percent. The decade of the 1960s began with rates around 2.0 percent and ended up with rates as high as 9.19 percent in October 1969. The 1970s saw declining interest rates to 3.9 percent in February 1972, then increasing to 12.92 percent in July 1974, then dropping to 4.77 percent in February 1976, and increasing again to 13.78 percent in December 1979.

Early in the 1980s rates jumped again sharply to 19.08 percent in January 1981 and stayed over 10.0 percent until September 1982. We were paying as much as 22.0 percent for loans in real estate. Not many businesses could stay healthy in this environment of record interest rates. Rates stayed high for the balance of the 1980s, averaging between 8.0 and 10.0 percent, with a short period between 1986 and 1987 when rates dropped briefly just below 5.0 percent.

The Bush administration inherited the beginning of a recession orchestrated by the Federal Reserve Board. The Fed's bellwether federal funds rate stands now at a forty-five-year low of 1.0 percent, after a steep easing cycle that began in January 2001, when the economy was entering a mild recession and the key lending rate stood at 6.5 percent.

The Federal Reserve Board hopes that the economy will pick up, helped by a $350 billion tax cut, lots of liquidity, and dollar depreciation. The June 25th drop in interest rates is insurance for the resumption of economic growth.

As you can see, it's important to follow closely what the Fed is up to. If the Fed is creating more money than the economy needs, it creates inflation with increase in prices. On the other hand, deflation means declining prices, because the Fed is creating a situation that results in a shortage of money.

3

COMMERCIAL BANKS

THIS SECTION FOCUSES on depository institutions consisting of commercial banks, savings institutions, credit unions, foreign banking, and other functions related to depository banking.

Opportunities

Numerous job opportunities exist among the two million or so financial positions held by people working in commercial banking. Table 3.1 lists just some of the positions available and the difference in mean salary over the course of two years for each.

Opportunities for employment during recent years have expanded greatly in the banking field. Beginning with the greater use of computers in the 1960s, banks have been able to perform both traditional and new services for customers faster and more efficiently.

Banks have also found that they can provide for businesses and individuals a whole range of services that were not even thought of

Table 3.1 Commercial Banks, Selected Business and Financial Operations, Occupations, Mean Annual Salaries for 1999 and 2001

Occupation Title	1999	2001	Annual Percent Change
Loan Officers	$47,800	$50,040	2.3
Cost Estimators	56,360	59,040	2.4
Management Analysts	55,580	60,310	4.3
Accountants and Auditors	43,890	46,130	2.6
Budget Analysts	51,550	55,480	3.8
Credit Analysts	41,650	46,020	5.3
Financial Analysts	49,220	56,800	7.7
Personal Financial Advisors	53,040	63,740	10.1
Financial Examiners	52,430	50,800	−1.6
Loan Counselors	37,540	37,820	0.4
Total	48,900	52,618	3.8

Source: U.S. Department of Labor, Bureau of Labor Statistics, SIC 602—Commercial Banks: bls.gov

a few years ago. For instance, banks today perform such services as doing payroll for businesses and sending out monthly statements for professionals.

Size of the Commercial Bank Industry

At the end of 1990, a total of 15,162 commercial banks were operating with 69,216 branches in the United States—a total of 84,378 offices. The year 2000 was the first time in more than sixty years that the number of banks dropped to only 9,904, and in 2001 to 9,513. However, the number of branches continued to rise to 76,748, bringing the total offices to 86,261. By 2005 it is estimated that the number of banks will drop further to about 8,900, but the number of branches will continue to increase to 80,100 and the total number of offices to 89,000.

Commercial banks employ close to 1.5 million people. In spite of the decline in the number of commercial banks and a small increase in the number of branches, bank assets exploded. Banks' assets increased by 77 percent from $1.86 million in 1980 to $3.3 trillion in 1990, and by 236 percent from $3.3 trillion in 1990 to $7.8 trillion in 2003. The main reasons for the decline in individual banks were the consolidation of banks, explosion of new technologies, changes in the financial institutions, expansion of e-mail traffic, banks offering drive-in facilities, automatic teller machines (ATMs), home computer banking (online banking), and full-service banking six days a week.

Consolidations have increased the number of branches and total offices to record levels. The growth in modern technology in the form of automated teller machines and online banking will likely have a decelerating effect on branch expansion. Consolidation of banks is not limited to the United States. For instance, Germany had 4,719 banks in 1970, 4,200 in 1992, and only 2,695 in 2001, a drop of 35.9 percent. Still, the number of branches continued to increase during that period by 30 percent to 63,834. Also the number of foreign branches increased from 391 in 1970 to 753 in 2001.

Texas leads in the number of banks with 839, followed by Illinois with 784 and Minnesota with 520. Employment in commercial banks will continue to increase at a pace slightly above that for most occupations to the year 2005.

The size of commercial banks has also grown considerably in the last two decades. Relaxed legal restrictions on geographic expansion and on the products banks can offer have significantly altered the structure of American banking. Expedited by the Riegle-Neal Act, banks have expanded beyond their traditional geographic borders, established by the McFadden Act of 1927 and the Douglas

Amendment of 1956. Interstate banks have united entire regions, thus providing tremendous flexibility to consumers.

As the American financial system continues into the era of financial conglomerates, banks, through mergers, takeovers, and failures, are entering the era of the megabank. The entry into banking functions of such disparate financial institutions as brokerage firms and insurance companies has intensified competition for traditional commercial banks, but experts predict that the largest of all three institutions will become financial supermarkets, offering virtually every category of financial service.

When the era of financial deregulation began, it was feared that many small banks would be driven out of business; to some extent there has been a noticeable drop in smaller banks and some increase in major banks. The high yielding money market accounts that became available in December 1982 were expected to lure small-town depositors out of the low-interest savings and checking accounts on which many small banks depend heavily.

In fact, however, many small-town banks have confounded the analysts by showing a great deal of resilience. Their customers have continued to leave billions of dollars in low- or no-interest accounts. Some little banks also have maintained their profit margins by raising loan rates and service charges.

This is not to suggest that small-town banks do not have problems. One major problem is their loss of affluent customers, whether individuals or institutions. Another is that smaller banks seem to be hit harder than large- or medium-sized banks in their rate of loan losses. The rate of loss is sometimes 50 percent higher than that of big banks. This has reduced the small banks' return on equity.

In addition, smaller banks with less than $100 million in assets have the lowest ratio of return of assets—0.91 compared to a total of 1.16; the lowest return on equity—8.07 versus 13.10 for all banks; and the highest percentage of banks losing money—11.2 percent versus 7.5 percent for all banks. Most profitable are the largest banks with assets in excess of $1 billion.

Nonetheless, the outlook for small banks in terms of financial viability, and, therefore, employment opportunities, is bright largely because of their strong relationships with depositors and their continued abundance of low-cost deposits. In contrast to larger metropolitan areas, where young urban professionals as well as retirees shop around for a bank with the highest interest rates, small towns still have many people who, for various reasons, stay with a low-paying local bank.

Besides loyal customers, many small-town banks have other advantages. Costs are managed well and marketing needs remain small because of sparse competition.

This does not mean to suggest that small banks are holding their own. On the contrary, smaller banks, capitalized with less than $100 million, lost some 1,367 banks between 1997 and 2001, while the largest banks gained 304 banks.

Commercial banking includes all services to businesses, farms, schools, churches, labor unions, other banks, and other organizations in need of any type of banking service. Commercial banks do a lot more than just make short- and long-term business loans to organizations. The various departments of a commercial bank provide billing services, prepare payroll checks, keep payroll records, and provide other services such as the transfer of funds and currency exchanges for international commerce. Some other financial careers available in commercial banking are in the following areas:

- **Coordinating services.** These are services provided by a larger bank to a smaller one. For example, the larger bank holds responsibility for all aspects of a customer's relationship with a correspondent bank, manages account relationships and exchanges of services between banks, and develops new accounts in different parts of the country where the bank wants to expand services.

- **Branch management.** A branch manager has complete responsibility for the operation and profitability of the branch bank, oversees the branch bank's staff, and may do some hiring of employees.
- **Operations.** The operations department oversees nonfee-based (nonloan) services such as foreign currency exchange, money transfers, and letters of credit. Management and line supervisory positions hold responsibility for supervising the clerical staff, making work assignments, establishing time schedules, training new employees, evaluating performance, and solving customer account problems.

Trust Banking

Trust banking involves an arrangement (or trust) in which one person or organization holds and manages property owned by another entity. The most common kinds of trusts include established wills and those set up by corporations for pensions or profit-sharing plans. In both cases, the bank trust officer manages the money or other property as if he or she owned it, paying out the proceeds of investments to the beneficiary as instructed by the terms of the trust. Bank trust departments also act as administrators of wills.

In addition to bank trust officers, trust account administrators explain new trusts to clients or to beneficiaries of the trust fund and administer estates by distributing property according to the terms of the will. Trust investment officers have the responsibility for investing money and any other property held in the trust, to earn the greatest possible return on the owner's investment. The trust officer adjusts stocks, bonds, and other investments and maintains a client's investments with an understanding of the goals of the trust and within the guidelines of the investment philosophy of the particular bank.

The administrative department of a bank provides services for the bank's internal operations. The accounting department maintains records required of any type of business, explains them and other financial data to management and stockholders, and draws conclusions about the financial health of the bank and its operations.

Foreign Banks in the United States

After an increase during the 1970s and 1980s, the number of foreign bank offices in the United States had slipped to 629 in 1995, from approximately 675 at the beginning of that decade. Branches and agencies made up 525 of these. Since then the activity of foreign banks strengthened as indicated by a recovery of their total assets to $1.4 trillion in 2002 from $1.3 trillion in 2000. Nearly half of these offices were located in New York, followed by California, Florida, and Illinois. The best-represented countries included Japan, the United Kingdom, and Canada. Assets of Japanese branches and agencies comprised almost 50 percent of all foreign assets, which account for over 16 percent of all U.S. banking assets. Like their American counterparts, foreign banks tend to hire locally rather than import employees, except perhaps in the highest levels of management, where executive officers are often natives of the country operating the U.S. office.

The share of total assets of New York foreign banks increased sharply. In 1973 their total share of deposits was 6.3 percent and by 1994 it had increased to 62.8 percent. It declined to 53.9 percent in 2002. Total assets increased from $22.2 billion in 1973 to $993.8 billion in 2002.

Overall assets of foreign banks in the United States increased from $32.3 billion to $1.34 trillion in 2002. Their shares jumped from 1.7 percent to 14.8 percent, with a peak of 18.3 percent in 1994.

The growth of emerging markets, the collapse of the Iron Curtain, and the resurgence of market economies increased banking's globalization in the 1990s. In 1993, Federal Reserve member banks were operating 1,361 branches in foreign countries and overseas areas of the United States, a net increase of 60 percent from 1989.

As of 2001, total assets of foreign banks in the United States stood at $1.30 trillion, a 75 percent increase from 1990, but its share of total domestic banks actually dropped slightly to 20.2 percent from the peak of 21.7 percent in 1995.

Bank Examiners

The Federal Deposit Insurance Corporation (FDIC) and the National Credit Union Savings Insurance Fund (NCUSIF) agencies of the United States government that insure bank deposits employ a vast regiment of bank examiners. Bank examiners are the chief guardians against bank failures. They look for violations of the law or of banking regulations and the existence of unsafe and unusual banking practices; they also assess a bank's internal procedures and determine its financial condition. After assembling and analyzing the data, the bank examiner discusses the findings with the bank's management and makes appropriate recommendations. The experienced bank examiner usually performs some auditing functions.

The trainee examiner is assigned as a member of a team of examiners. With experience, the trainee moves from simpler tasks to more difficult assignments. The latter include test audits, preparation of schedules of earnings, audits of expenses and capital accounts, classification and appraisal of assets, and analysis of specific problems and their solutions. In addition there are about six thousand financial examiners employed by depository institutions; their salaries average $55,000 annually.

Working Conditions

The job of a bank examiner requires frequent travel, although the degree of travel varies from region to region. For the most part, the extent of travel is more pronounced in rural areas than in larger metropolitan ones. It may also be necessary for the bank examiner to relocate from one duty station to another within a given region.

Training and Education

Most trainees join the FDIC or NCUSIF directly out of college upon earning a bachelor's degree or, more often, a graduate degree. The academic background must include a minimum of twenty-four semester hours, or their equivalent, in finance, economics, business administration, or accounting. At least 50 percent of these semester hours must be in accounting subjects. Three years of banking or bank examining experience can substitute for these educational qualifications. To qualify, banking experience must include work in the following areas:

- Accounting or auditing in a bank (requires knowledge of debits and credits, balance sheets, and operating statements)

- Analyzing and recommending investment
- Reviewing, recommending, or approving loan applications or investments

Current Employment

Bank examiners have traditionally accounted for a large group of the employees of the FDIC. However, with greater stability in the banking industry and a decreasing number of bank failures, the number of bank examiners is going to be reduced. Within the FDIC, the number of bank examiners is fewer than three thousand. The Office of Thrift Supervision, the National Credit Union Administration, and bank regulatory offices in the various states also employ bank examiners.

Promotions and entrance salaries are based on the employee's training, experience, and ability. The examiner starts out as a Grade 5 trainee. After twelve months of satisfactory service, the trainee examiner may be advanced to assistant, or Grade 7. The next level is that of assistant examiner. A variety of assignments and advanced training determine how far an examiner can advance.

Bank Failures No Longer a Problem

The chances that you may lose a job because of bank failures such as those so prominent at the end of the last century are small to nil. The FDIC maintains a list of problem banks as part of its bank monitoring effort. As of the end of 2001, the number of problem banks had fallen to one, down significantly from 280 in 1988. This compares to 506 failed banks in 1921, 1,390 in 1930, 2,293 in 1931, 1,493 in 1932, and 4,000 in 1933. The peak in losses to depositors of almost $7 billion was reached in 1988 and the second peak of just over $6 billion in 1991. In 1988 only $2.6 million was ever recovered, but in 1991 that figure rose to $723.3 billion.

Since 1980 banks carry a $100,000 deposit insurance, a substantial increase from the $5,000 per deposit that existed between 1934 and 1949. Money today is quite safe.

Even if a bank fails, there is a substantial recovery to the insuring agency, the FDIC. In the upheaval during the financial crisis of the 1980s, when gross loss reached $12.1 billion in 1988, the net loss was reduced by recoveries to $6.9 billion. In cases of bank failures, the two principal methods available to the FDIC to protect depositors are deposit payoffs and deposit assumptions.

One way to measure the stability of the banking system is to compare the charge-off rates and delinquency rates. Charge-offs, which are the value of loans removed from the books and charged against loss reserves, are measured net of recoveries as a percentage of average loans and are annualized. Delinquent loans are those past due thirty days or more and still accruing interest, as well as those in nonaccrual status. They are measured as a percentage of end-of-period loans.

Looking at the data since 1985 to mid-1991, both measures changed substantially upward during the economic downturn. The charge-off rate jumped by 118.7 percent, from 0.80 percent to 1.75 percent, mostly due to increases in the credit card charge-off from 2.02 percent to 4.92 percent. At the same time the charge-off on commercial real estate also increased from 0.91 percent to 2.40 percent. From then on, charge-off rates declined to 0.42 percent in the last quarter of 1994 and stayed below the 1.0 percent level until the last quarter of 2001. They reached 1.14 percent the first quarter of 2002 and have declined since to 0.90 percent.

Similarly, the total delinquency rates on loans and leases peaked at 5.48 percent in 1987 and again at 6.15 percent in 1991, then dropped to 2.04 percent at the end of 1999 and began to increase slightly to 2.58 percent at the end of 2002.

Clearly both data indicate a strong banking position with charge-off rates at only 0.13 percent on residential properties and 0.13 percent on commercial properties. Even a credit card write-off peaked at 7.67 percent in the first quarter of 2002; it is now down to 5.43 percent.

Industry Outlook

The economic expansion and diversification of banking services of the 1990s has meant a healthy growth in commercial banking. Borrowing demand by commercial and industrial institutions is expected to continue to grow, as well as credit card lending to individuals. Commercial banks reported record earnings in 2001, growing almost 6 percent over 1994's previous record. In 1990 the return on assets was 0.48 percent, and in 2001 it was 1.16 percent.

You can determine the financial health of a bank on the website bankrate.com, which rates more than ten thousand FDIC-insured banks and thrifts and twelve thousand credit unions. It rates financial institutions as weak, below industry average, performing, sound, and superior. Ratings are based on capitalization, assets quality, earnings, and liquidity. Some banks post this information on their own websites.

According to Web Census 2002, a joint survey of the ABA Banking Journal and the ABA Community Bankers Council released on March 4, 2003, nearly one in five bankers predicts that the Internet will be the leading consumer banking channel by 2005.

Banks' Performance Continues to Outstrip 2001 Results

Through the first nine months of 2002, commercial banks earned $68.6 billion, up $12.9 billion (23.2 percent) from the same period in 2001. The industry's return on assets at the latter part of 2003 was 1.37 percent, compared to 1.17 percent in the first three quarters of 2001. Almost three out of every four banks (72.6 percent) reported improved year-to-date earnings. The main source of the earnings improvement was higher net interest income (up $19.3 billion, or 12.2 percent). Net interest margins were above the levels of 2002, and interest-earning assets grew by 6.2 percent. These improvements, along with a $10.8 billion (9.2 percent) increase in noninterest income, outweighed a $7.2 billion (25.6 percent) rise in provisions for loan losses. Almost half of the increase in loss provisions in 2003 (46.6 percent) was in banks' international operations.

4

SAVINGS INSTITUTIONS

SAVINGS INSTITUTIONS SERVE as a link between people who have funds to save or invest and those who want to borrow. A savings institution accepts savings deposits from the public, and then uses these funds to make various types of loans. Most of its investments are in residential real estate mortgages and particularly in loans on owner-occupied single-family homes.

Opportunities

Of the 1,467 savings and loans, the state with the largest number was Massachusetts (175), followed by Ohio (116), Pennsylvania (110), Illinois (110), New York (75), New Jersey (69), Indiana (60), Maryland (56), Florida (41), and California (39).

In terms of employees the ten largest states were as follows: California 67,058, New York 22,675, Pennsylvania 22,343, Massachusetts 15,926, Washington 14,696, Virginia 12,696, Texas 11,954, Connecticut 11,497, Ohio 9,795, and New Jersey 9,251.

Table 4.1 shows the mean annual salaries of employees working in the eight major financial occupations in savings institutions for 1999 and 2001. As you can see, between 1999 and 2001 salaries increased by 5.2 percent annually to $47,540. The highest paid occupation among this group was personal financial advisors and the lowest was loan counselors.

The same group of workers' salaries compared well with credit union employees, but was lower than that of commercial bank or foreign bank employees.

History

The first U.S. savings and loan association was founded in 1831. In 1932 the Federal Home Loan Bank System was created to oversee the savings and loan associations, with deposits to be insured by the Federal Savings and Loan Insurance Corporation (FSLIC). Since 1933 the federal government has chartered savings and loan

Table 4.1 Savings Institutions, Selected Business and Financial Operations, Occupations, Mean Annual Salaries for 1999 and 2001

Occupation Title	1999	2001	Annual Percent Change
Management Analysts	$53,040	$53,450	1.3
Accountants and Auditors	41,870	44,430	3.2
Budget Analysts	47,510	55,250	8.1
Credit Analysts	38,970	44,220	7.7
Financial Analysts	51,760	54,610	2.7
Personal Financial Advisors	43,610	57,770	16.0
Financial Examiners	46,230	48,920	2.9
Loan Counselors	34,020	35,970	2.8
Total	43,070	47,540	5.2

Source: U.S. Department of Labor, Bureau of Labor Statistics, SIC 603: bls.gov

associations. After World War II, the associations began a period of rapid expansion.

Savings and loan institutions went through many changes in recent years, primarily due to deregulatory measures instituted in the 1980s by the U.S. federal government, allowing them to offer a much wider range of services than ever before. The deregulatory measures allowed savings and loan associations to enter the business of commercial lending, trust services, and nonmortgage consumer lending. The Depository Institutions Deregulation/Monetary Control Act of 1980 began these sweeping changes.

Savings institutions are traditionally exposed to a high level of risk because of the unbalanced nature of their portfolios. On average, three-fourths of savings and loan assets were invested in mortgage loans, but the Garn St. Germain Act passed in the early 1980s allowed savings and loans to offer everything from checking accounts to consumer and commercial loans. The concentration of assets in home mortgages, the customary market niche, dropped from 72.6 percent in 1978 to 53.6 percent in 1986, just prior to the advent of serious problems for the industry.

Savings institutions were among the businesses most heavily affected by the Tax Reform Act of 1986. Wide variations in operating performance and management, as well as regional economic downturns, also had significant impact on the stability of some institutions within the industry.

The Federal Savings and Loan Insurance Corporation and the Federal Deposit Insurance Corporation (FDIC) were established in the early 1930s to insure deposits at savings associations and savings banks and at commercial banks. (During their years of operation, both the FSLIC and the FDIC have accumulated a good deal of reserves.) Two years later, the Depository Institutions Act gave savings and loan institutions the right to make secured and unsecured loans to a wide range of markets, permitted developers to own savings and loan associations, and allowed owners of these institutions to lend to themselves. Under the new laws, the Federal Home Loan Bank Board (FHLBB) was given a number of new powers to secure the capital positions of the savings and loan associations. Under these new laws, the FHLBB allowed savings and loan associations to "print their own capital" and escape charges of insolvency through such measures as "goodwill," in which customer loyalty and market share were counted as part of a capital base. As a result, a thrift that was technically insolvent could resist government seizure. This was the beginning of the collapse, caused by Congress.

Savings and loan associations began to engage in large-scale speculation, particularly in real estate. Financial failure of the institutions became rampant, with well over five hundred forced to close during the 1980s. In 1989, after the FSLIC itself became insolvent, the FDIC took over the FSLIC's insurance obligations, and the Resolution Trust Corporation was created to buy and sell defaulted savings and loan associations. The Office of Thrift Supervision was also created in an attempt to identify struggling savings and loan organizations before it was too late. The cost to U.S. government—that is, taxpayers—was more than $500 billion over thirty years to bail out the savings and loan associations.

Severe financial pressures caused by faltering institutions depleted the FSLIC's reserves in the 1980s. In late 1988, FSLIC-assisted bailouts of troubled institutions began to accelerate dramatically. By the end of the year, the FSLIC counted more than 365 problem cases. Legislation enacted by Congress authorized funds to cover the savings-and-loan bailout. The act to assist savings and loan associations established the Resolution Trust Corporation (RTC) to help in liquidating insolvent institutions and their assets by 1995. Within six years the RTC resolved all 747 institutions taken under its control, recovering 87 percent of book value. The FDIC succeeded the RTC.

Size of Savings Institutions

Since 1990 the number of savings institutions dropped from 2,815 to 1,534 in 2001, but the net assets increased from a low of $1.026 billion in 1995 to $1.359 billion in 2002. As of 2003 the number of savings and loans have stabilized with an annual increase in assets estimated at 7 percent. Savings institutions are expected to have increased their assets portfolio by 2005 to $1.41 billion. Savings institutions employed 258,000 in 2002, with 150,000 in federal institutions and 108,000 in state institutions.

Like the commercial banking system, the savings institution business has a dual system of chartering and supervision. State institutions are chartered under state statutes and are supervised and examined by their respective state authorities. Federal associations are chartered under the provisions of the Home Owners' Loan Act and are subject to the supervision of the Office of Thrift Supervision (OTS), formerly the Federal Home Loan Bank Board.

The Federal Home Loan Bank System

The Federal Home Loan Bank System was created in 1932 to provide a central credit facility for the nation's home-financing institutions. The savings institution system links mortgage-lending institutions to the capital markets by issuing consolidated obligations and discount notes in large denominations. The system also serves as a source of secondary liquidity to its members in meeting heavy or unusual withdrawal demands.

The system is organized in a manner similar to the Federal Reserve System. It is composed of the Office of Thrift Supervision, the twelve regional bank districts, and the member institutions.

A new era for savings institutions began in August 1989 with the signing of the Financial Institutions Reform, Recovery, and Enforcement Act of 1989 (FIRREA). This act provided $50 billion to close failed savings institutions, completely changed the regulatory apparatus for the industry, and legislated a number of new portfolio constraints. The act strongly reaffirmed the mission of savings institutions to be residential mortgage lenders, recognizing that much of the trouble began with expanded lending that dangerously reduced the capital-to-deposit ratio.

The Federal Home Loan Bank Board was abolished under the act, and in its place the Office of Thrift Supervision, a new bureau of the Treasury Department, regulates the activities of the thrift industry.

All federally insured savings and loan associations are required by law to belong to the OTS system. Membership is open on a voluntary basis to qualified state-chartered savings associations, mutual savings banks, and life insurance companies.

District Banks

The district banks carry out the functions of the OTS in its dealings with member institutions. Although they are part of the federal government, they are wholly owned by their member institutions.

Each bank has its own staff and board of directors. Each board is composed of six directors appointed by the OTS for four-year terms, plus an additional number of directors elected for two-year terms by member institutions.

The regional banks are not autonomous. Besides governing them and setting systemwide policies, the OTS reviews their annual budgets and must approve appointments of top personnel.

The banks provide many services to members besides deposit facilities and advances. Among these services are the safekeeping, purchase, and sale of securities, and the operation of statistical and research programs that trace economic conditions in the particular bank district.

Savings Institutions Are Strong Holders of Mortgages

In addition to banks, savings and loans, and credit unions, there are several federal and related agencies and mortgage pools and trusts that deal in and hold mortgages. At the end of 2001, mortgage pools and trusts held $3.698 trillion in mortgage debt. This was 48.7 percent of the total debt of $7.596 trillion. The federal and related agencies held $377 billion, or 5 percent. Of the total debt, 81.5 percent was in residential real estate, 16.9 percent was in non-residential real estate, and 1.6 percent was in farm real estate.

Total U.S. mortgage debt increased from $3.9 trillion to $7.6 trillion, or by 94.4 percent from 1990 to 2001, an increase of 8.6 percent annually. Of this, one-family home mortgages jumped by 116.4 percent from $2.65 trillion to $5.74 trillion. The share of single-family debt increased since 1990 from 67.9 percent to 75.6 percent. The sharpest increase among private holders by institutions holding mortgage debt were commercial banks, jumping by 111.4 percent. Both savings and loans and life insurance companies have seen a drop in mortgage debt.

Holders of mortgages by mortgage pools and trusts increased well over threefold from $1.09 trillion to $3.69 trillion. Of this, Federal National Mortgage Association (Fannie Mae) debt skyrocketed from $300 billion to $1.29 trillion. The Federal Home Loan Mortgage Corporation (Freddie Mac) is a wholly owned corporate instrument of the U.S. government, operating within the Housing and Urban Development department (HUD). The Government National Mortgage Association (GNMA), or Ginnie Mae, was created in 1968 to assume certain functions formerly belonging to Fannie Mae, as well as to guarantee securities backed by mortgages insured or guaranteed by the federal government.

The pass-through is the major type of Ginnie Mae guaranteed mortgage-backed security issued by private mortgage lenders. It provides for passing along to the security holder the monthly payments of interest and principal on the underlying pool of mortgages. The security is fully guaranteed by the federal government.

Industry Trends: Strong Recovery After Crisis

In 1997 the Office of Thrift Supervision reported that for the first time since its inception none of the thrifts that it regulates were considered "seriously troubled." "Other troubled institutions" comprised a list of thirty-two thrifts, 2.4 percent of the 1,334 thrifts regulated by the OTS. Assets in troubled thrifts fell to 1.17 percent of total assets in 1996.

As of March 31, 2003, there were 1,450 FDIC savings institutions, slightly less than the 1,467 in 2002. As of March 31, 2003, total assets were $1.46 trillion, up slightly from the total assets of $1.4 on March 31, 2002.

Savings institutions are diversifying, yet they continue to be dominated by home mortgages. Small business and consumer loans are the fastest-growing segments of the loan portfolio.

5

CREDIT UNIONS

CREDIT UNIONS ARE nonprofit financial cooperatives organized solely to meet the needs of their members. Like the savings and loan associations, the credit unions of today look so much like banks that it is sometimes difficult to tell the difference. They offer the same consumer services, from checking and savings accounts to credit cards and home mortgage loans. One major difference is that there is not a commercial finance department in a credit union because these institutions are owned and directed by their members.

Opportunities

According to the National Credit Unions Association (NCUA), credit union membership grew in 2001 by 2.3 percent to reach 79,377,000 members, and savings increased 14 percent to $530 billion. Credit union loans also grew 6 percent to $393 billion. As of 2001 there were 6,118 federal and 3,866 state credit units. The share of state credit unions in 2001 was 24.8 percent, substantially down from 36.2 percent in 1990.

In 2001 credit unions employed 192,000 workers, up 4.3 percent from 184,000 in 1999. The total assets jumped by 14.4 percent to $501.5 billion, from $438.2 billion in 2000.

Table 5.1 shows nine occupations available at credit unions and their mean annual wages for 1999 and 2001. The wages increased at 3.4 percent annually to $34,960, with management analysts making the highest wages at $47,580 and loan counselors the lowest at $28,470.

A credit union is a cooperative financial institution that is owned and controlled by the people who use its services. These people are members. Credit unions serve groups that share something in common, such as where they work, live, or go to church. Credit unions are not-for-profit and exist to provide a safe, convenient place for members to save money and to get loans at reasonable rates.

Table 5.1 Credit Unions, Selected Business and Financial Operations, Occupations, Mean Annual Salaries for 1999 and 2001

Occupation Title	1999	2001	Annual Percent Change
Management Analysts	$43,990	$47,580	4.1
Accountants and Auditors	35,039	38,690	5.2
Budget Analysts	34,850	43,930	13.0
Credit Analysts	39,930	34,460	5.5
Financial Analysts	41,300	44,840	4.3
Personal Financial Advisors	33,090	42,010	13.5
Financial Examiners	40,520	40,120	−0.5
Loan Counselors	29,700	28,470	−2.1
Loan Officers	32,210	33,310	1.7
Total	32,710	34,960	3.4

Source: U.S. Department of Labor, Bureau of Labor Statistics, SIC 606: bls.gov

Nationwide there are about eleven thousand credit unions worth $480 billion and serving seventy-nine million members, claims the credit association. Karen Dorway, president and the director of research at Bauer Financial in Coral Gables, Florida, said one factor in the proliferation of credit unions and banks in general in recent years is due to an outflow of money from the stock market. "The number of deposits at banks and credit unions is up over the last several years," Ms. Dorway said. She also said another reason more credit unions could be moving to the county is because of changes in legislation and regulations. "In order to become members of a particular credit union you have to meet certain qualifications," Ms. Dorway said. "But the capacity to become a member (of a credit union) has become more broad over the past several years. There are still limitations, but they're not as definitive as they once were."

A Brief History of Credit Unions

The credit union idea is a simple one: People pool their money and make loans to each other. It's an idea that evolved from cooperative activities in the nineteenth century in Europe.

Since that time, credit unions' guiding principles have remained the same: (1) only people who are credit union members should borrow there; (2) loans are made for "prudent and productive" purposes; and (3) a person's desire to repay (character) is considered more important than the ability (income) to repay. Members are, after all, borrowing their own money and that of their friends.

At the beginning of the twentieth century, the credit union idea surfaced in Canada. Canada's successful efforts profoundly influenced two Americans: Pierre Jay, the Massachusetts banking commissioner, and Edward A. Filene, a Boston merchant.

These two men helped organize public hearings on credit union legislation in Massachusetts, leading to passage of the first state credit union act in 1909. Growth was slow, however. Fewer than ten states passed credit union laws, many of them unworkable. The Massachusetts Credit Union Association grew slowly.

The 1970s brought major changes in the products offered by financial institutions, and credit unions found that they, too, needed to expand their services. In 1977, legislation brought expanded services to credit union members, including share certificates and mortgage lending. In 1979, a three-member board replaced the NCUA administrator. In the same year, Congress created the Central Liquidity Facility, the credit union lender of last resort. The 1970s were years of tremendous growth in credit unions. The number of credit union members more than doubled and assets in credit unions tripled to more than $65 billion.

Credit unions have been around since about the turn of the nineteenth century, but in 1934 the federal credit union system was inaugurated under legislation signed by President Franklin Roosevelt. By 1942, four thousand credit unions with more than one million members were part of the national system. In 1948, Congress created the Bureau of Federal Credit Unions within the Federal Security Administration. Between 1953 and 1970, federal credit unions doubled, and membership almost quadrupled.

Deregulation, increased flexibility in merger and field of membership criteria, and expanded member services characterized the 1980s. High interest rates and unemployment in the early 1980s brought supervisory changes and insurance losses. With the Share Insurance Fund near bankruptcy, the credit union community called on Congress to approve a plan to recapitalize the fund.

In 1985, federally insured credit unions recapitalized the National Credit Union Share Insurance Fund (NCUSIF) by depositing 1 percent of their shares into the Share Insurance Fund. Backed by the "full faith and credit of the United States Government," the NCUSIF has three "fail-safe" features:

- Federal credit unions must maintain a 1 percent deposit in the fund.
- Premiums are levied by the board, if necessary.
- When the equity ratio exceeds 1.3 percent ($1.30 on deposit for every $100 insured), the board sends a dividend to credit unions.

Since the recapitalization, the NCUA board has only charged credit unions a premium once. In 1991 the fund dropped to a 1.23 percent equity level, and credit unions were asked to pay a premium. During the 1990s, credit unions were healthy and growing. Membership increased from 36.24 million in 1990 to 44 million in 2003.

Organization

Each credit union is governed by its membership. Members elect unpaid, volunteer officers and directors who establish the credit union's policies. Voting within credit unions is democratic. In banks and savings and loan associations, only stockholders in the corporation have voting power, not the average account holder. In the credit union system, all are voting members regardless of the size of their accounts.

Credit unions are typically organized around a particular field of membership, primarily employee groups, associations, religious or fraternal affiliations, or residential areas. Through cooperative effort among credit unions at local, state, and national levels, many credit unions of all sizes offer their members a broad array of financial services. These include preauthorized bill payment, money orders, safe deposit boxes, remedial financial counseling, ATM cards, credit cards, share drafts (checking), IRAs, traveler's checks, money market accounts, trust accounts, home equity credit, home mortgage loans, home improvement loans, guaranteed student loans, and wire transfer of funds. In some larger institutions, formal financial planning, discount brokerage, and auto leasing are among the available services.

Although most credit unions are chartered with the NCUA and federally insured by the NCUSIF, several thousand others are insured by their states, with only a few remaining uninsured.

The NCUSIF has prospered in the 1990s as the health and growth rates of credit unions have improved. The statistic indicating the health of a financial institution is the ratio of capital to deposits or shares. As of 1995, the capital ratio for the NCUSIF-insured credit unions was 10.3 percent, compared to 8.1 percent for savings institutions. High capital ratios and support of the NCUSIF have helped credit union failures decline throughout the 1990s. In 1980, 239 credit institutions out of 17,350 failed. The number declined to 164 in 1990, 26 in 1995, and 22 in 2001.

The crisis affecting the savings and loans also touched credit unions, but to a lesser degree due to better capital ratios. Failures in the 1970s and 1980s were mainly in small, single-group credit unions. The Financial Institution Reform, Recovery, and Enforcement Act of 1989 significantly expanded the enforcement powers of U.S. regulatory agencies, including the NCUA. The NCUA responded by combining smaller credit unions into large multigroup institutions. However, later consolidations were approved that were not connected to either financial problems or a common bond.

Industry Outlook

The outlook for credit unions remains reasonably bullish. There is little chance that the upheaval of the past will be repeated. Credit unions, like other financial institutions, are closely regulated. The National Credit Union Share Insurance Fund, administered by the National Credit Union Administration, an agency of the federal government, insures deposits of credit union members at more than eleven thousand federal and state-chartered credit unions nationwide. Deposits are insured up to $100,000.

What makes a credit union different from a bank or savings and loan? Like credit unions, banks and savings and loans accept deposits and make loans, but unlike credit unions, they are in business to make a profit. Banks and savings and loans are owned by groups of stockholders whose interests include earning a healthy return on their investments.

The deregulation of credit unions coupled with rapid growth of assets, membership, and services continued throughout the 1990s and beyond. Membership continues to increase, thereby requiring additional employees to serve the needs of a growing market.

For potential employees, credit union management emphasizes education, skills, team performance, and strategic planning abilities. More complex services and products require a higher level of managerial sophistication.

Traditional credit unions nationwide employ fewer than two hundred thousand workers. Most of these employees work in institutions that have assets of more than $5 million. The types of positions available at credit unions are essentially the same required in all financial institutions, including tellers, loan officers, financial managers, and analysts.

6

OTHER TYPES OF NONDEPOSITORY FINANCIAL INSTITUTIONS

ALTHOUGH COMMERCIAL BANKS, savings and loan associations, and credit unions comprise the majority of banking institutions, there are a number of other organizations involved with the functions of financing. The federal government created nearly all of these other organizations in the middle of the twentieth century. They were set up for the purpose of helping stabilize the economy as well as to advance home ownership. Together, these industries account for approximately 9 percent of the total employment of deposit institutions. However, employment in these smaller organizations is supposed to grow by 30 percent in the next ten years. The U.S. Department of Labor describes four categories of financial institutions as nondepository credit institutions. They are: (1) federal and federally sponsored agencies, (2) personal credit institutions, (3) business credit institutions, and (4) mortgage bankers and brokers.

Opportunities

This group employs some 695,370 workers with approximately 28.8 percent, or 200,550 workers, employed by personal credit institutions; 18.5 percent, or 128,810 workers, employed by business credit institutions; 50.1 percent, or 348,590 workers, employed by mortgage bankers and brokers; and 2.6 percent, or 17,420 workers, employed by federal and federally sponsored agencies.

Table 6.1 lists eight occupations in nondepository credit institutions and their mean annual salaries for 1999 and 2001.

The Federal National Mortgage Association

As discussed earlier, Congress created the Federal National Mortgage Association (FNMA), called Fannie Mae, in 1938 to bolster home ownership during the Depression. Three decades later it was partially privatized but retained certain important government benefits. In 1970 Congress created another entity, Freddie Mac, to

Table 6.1 Federal and Federally Sponsored Credit Agencies, Selected Business and Financial Operations, Occupations, Mean Annual Salaries, 1999 and 2001

Occupation Title	1999	2001	Annual Percent Change
Management Analysts	$48,670	$60,970	12.8
Accountants and Auditors	46,050	49,160	3.4
Credit Analysts	46,440	49,670	3.5
Financial Analysts	42,990	54,060	12.8
Personal Financial Advisors	NA	83,500	NA
Financial Examiners	NA	53,030	NA
Loan Counselors	35,910	40,630	6.5
Tax Officers	46,550	51,180	5.0
Total	45,570	49,490	4.3

Source: U.S. Department of Labor, SIC 611—Commercial Banks: bls.gov

enlarge competition. Both are what are called "government sponsored agencies." This move expanded the pool of money for mortgages by buying loans and converting them into relatively safe mortgage-backed securities.

The basic function of the Federal National Mortgage Association is to provide a secondary market in residential loans. FNMA fulfills this function by buying, servicing, and selling mortgages. Both Fannie Mae and Freddie Mac were created to provide a continuous and low-cost source of credit to finance America's housing. Specifically, these Congress-approved corporations aim to increase the supply of funds that mortgage lenders, such as commercial banks, mortgage bankers, savings institutions, and credit unions, can make available to home buyers and multifamily investors. They make mortgages available to those who might not qualify for (or cannot afford) traditional loans.

For years Washington has tried to find a solution for the following scenario: When all goes well, both companies are allowed to keep the profit. But if nothing goes right, government steps in and pays for the losses. This is precisely what happened during the savings and loan crisis that resulted in a $500-billion bailout by the public. Critics have said for years that the two companies are building a "house of cards" by avoiding full public disclosure. Both companies have grown explosively in recent years.

In mid-June 2003, Freddie Mac fired its president, David Glenn, and its chairman and chief financial officers resigned among accounting troubles. With a strong growth, both companies decided to increase their business into so called "derivatives," a complex financial instrument to hedge interest rate risks. Derivatives played a major role in the collapse of Enron in 2001. Before that, in 1998, derivatives were behind the near-demise of hedge fund long-term capital management. On June 20, 2003, the *Wall Street Journal* reported that at the end of September 2002, Freddie Mac grew its derivatives-trading positions sharply up to nearly $700 billion, an increase of 46 percent from 2000.

Government Helps Both Institutions in Various Forms

Both companies are exempt from state and local income taxes. Their debt securities receive favorable regulatory treatment. They are eligible for the Federal Reserve Board open market transactions and are entitled to use the federal government's deposits of tax revenues as collateral. Consequently, financial markets regard them as extremely sound and accord them better rates than other corporations. The Congressional Budget Office estimates that these agencies received $13.6 billion in federal subsides. Of that, about half was passed on to mortgage borrowers as lower borrowing costs.

The government subsidy is the rationale used by those who oppose government subsidizing these institutions. They demand more government regulations and complain that much of the $7 billion left from the $13.6 billion each year ends up in the pockets of stockholders and management.

It is reasonable to think that these institutions are not about to fail; they are popular with the public and Congress in that they reduce mortgage costs and thus help home buyers, and they cut substantially and help to stabilize potential economic volatility. However, there is a serious question as to whether the U.S. government will step in to bail out these two institutions if they should fail.

Home Ownership Up Sharply

With the home-ownership rate at 67.8 percent in 2001 these institutions contributed strongly in bringing the home ownership share from 58.5 percent in 1970 to 59.5 percent in 1980, 66.7 percent in 1990, and 67.8 percent in 2001. According to recent statistics, of a total of 119.1 million housing units, 80.1 million are home owners. This is the highest share in the world, and some of it is the result of these two institutions.

In April 2003, Ford Company and Fannie Mae were rated among the top ten best companies for diversity by *Diversifying*, a magazine and website publisher. For diversity, retention, payments, and hiring, Fannie Mae rated second after the Ford Company.

Fannie Mae has been owned by private shareholders since 1968, although it still has a number of ties to the government. The President appoints five of Fannie Mae's fifteen directors. Mortgage debt held by FNMA increased from $300 billion in 1990 to $1.29 trillion in 2001.

Both agencies own or guarantee about 42 percent of the U.S. $7 trillion mortgage market, about one-third of all goods and services we produce annually. Many people are worried about their potential impact on the economy should anything like the savings and loan bailout occur. In July 2003, outside investigators uncovered improper accounting at Freddie Mac, triggering a major concern about financial markets.

Under the Bush plan, the Department of the Treasury would take over the regulatory beat from the Office of Federal Housing Enterprise Oversight. This will give the Department of the Treasury more power to check on the companies' risk-based capital standard, or how much capital both entities should have to withstand volatility.

The Bush Administration plan is opposed by the National Association of Home Builders: "NAHB strongly believes that Fannie Mae's and Freddie Mac's ability to spur innovative solutions and to develop new products that increase home ownership will continue only if the mission of these corporations is regulated by HUD."

This is simply not true. HUD has enough problems of its own and should concentrate on its own role in housing. So far, it has been totally incapable of looking after these two financial giants. Of any of the federal agencies, the Department of the Treasury should be monitoring Fannie Mae and Freddie Mac, and it would be responsible for a bailout in case they defaulted, not HUD.

Fannie Mae has five regional offices located in Chicago, Philadelphia, Atlanta, Dallas, and Pasadena. In addition, there are fifty-four partnership offices in every state. Fannie Mae's main office is in Washington, D.C. For more information, go to fanniemae.com.

Freddie Mac and Fannie Mae have the same charters, congressional mandates, and regulatory structure. However, the two companies have different business strategies. Competition between Freddie Mac and Fannie Mae ensures that the benefits of the secondary market are passed on to home buyers and renters in the form of lower housing costs. Both operate as publicly traded corporations. Both loans are referred to as conforming loans, since they conform to government service standards.

The Federal Home Loan Mortgage Corporation

As mentioned above, the Federal Home Loan Mortgage Corporation (FHLMC), popularly called Freddie Mac, was created to promote the flow of capital into the housing market by establishing an active secondary market in mortgages. The corporation is under the direction of an eighteen-member board and by law may deal only with government-supervised lenders.

Congress created Freddie Mac and Fannie Mae to buy home loans from banks and other lenders to supply ready cash to the home-mortgage market. They buy mortgages from lenders either to keep in their portfolios or package into securities for sale on Wall

Street. Investors from around the globe buy the securities, with a large amount of them held by Japanese and other Asian investors.

The FHLMC provides additional funds for loan to lenders by purchasing existing mortgages from their portfolios. The corporation's programs cover conventional mortgage loans of various types, participations in conventional loans, and FHA and VA loans.

Freddie Mac is a shareholder-owned corporation. The company links Main Street to Wall Street by purchasing, securing, and investing in home mortgages. This ultimately provides home owners and renters with lower housing costs and better access to home financing. Freddie Mac buys residential mortgages and funds them in the capital markets.

America has a secondary mortgage market, led by Freddie Mac, that attracts capital from around the world to finance a wide range of mortgage products designed specifically to make home ownership affordable and accessible. Freddie Mac conducts its business by buying mortgages that meet the company's underwriting and product standards from lenders, packaging the mortgages into securities, and selling the securities guaranteed by Freddie Mac to investors, such as insurance companies.

Freddie Mac (freddiemac.com) is a shareholder-owned corporation whose people are dedicated to improving the quality of life by making the American dream of decent, accessible housing a reality. Since its inception, Freddie Mac has achieved more than thirty consecutive years of profitability and has financed one out of every six homes in America. Freddie Mac employs thirty-nine hundred people. Freddie Mac's operating revenue at the end of 2001 was $5.88 billion; operating earnings were $3.2 billion, with net assets of $617.7 billion. Its revenues since 2001 jumped to $39.7 billion and pushed Freddie Mac to number thirty-two on the Fortune 500 list.

At the present time, both Fannie Mae and Freddie Mac are under investigation by Congress for their accounting practices. Federal Reserve Board Chairman Alan Greenspan insisted that both companies shouldn't be exempt from the public-disclosure requirements that apply to nearly all publicly traded companies. Says Greenspan, "There is no reason to differentiate Fannie Mae and Freddie Mac from the rest of the securities industry as far as I'm concerned."

The Government National Mortgage Association

The Government National Mortgage Association (GNMA), called Ginnie Mae (ginniemae.com), was created in 1968 as a wholly owned corporation within the Department of Housing and Urban Development (HUD). Its purpose was—and is—to serve low- to moderate-income home buyers.

The National Housing Act was enacted on June 27, 1934, as one of several economic recovery measures. It provided for the establishment of a Federal Housing Administration (FHA) to be headed by a Federal Housing Administrator. As one of the principal functions of the FHA, Title II of the act provided for the insurance of home mortgage loans made by private lenders.

Title III of the act provided for the chartering of national mortgage associations by the administrator. These associations were to be private corporations regulated by the administrator, and their chief purpose was to buy and sell the mortgages to be insured by FHA under Title II. Only one association was ever formed under this authority. It was formed on February 10, 1938, as a subsidiary of the Reconstruction Finance Corporation, a government corporation. Its name was National Mortgage Association of Washington, and this was changed that same year to Federal National Mortgage Association.

By amendments made in 1968, the Federal National Mortgage Association was partitioned into two separate entities, one to be known as Government National Mortgage Association (Ginnie Mae), the other to retain the name Federal National Mortgage Association. Ginnie Mae remained in the government, and Fannie Mae became privately owned by retiring the government-held stock. Ginnie Mae has operated as a wholly owned government association.

Revenues increased 4.1 percent in 2000 and 5.5 percent in 2001, while excess of revenues over expenses increased in 2000 by 2.1 percent and in 2001 by 5.5 percent. Total assets increased by 11.1 percent and 12.4 percent. Operating results for 2001 exceeded historic performance levels. Ginnie Mae's mortgage-backed securities have financed home ownership opportunities for 26.8 million American families.

The Department of Veterans Affairs

The U.S. Department of Veteran's Affairs (va.gov) was established in 1944 with the original GI Bill. Included in the many provisions was a program (homeloans.va.gov) to assist World War II veterans with the purchase of new homes. The assistance provided a guarantee of a portion of the mortgage loan to finance the purchase of a primary home. Most loans were low or no down payment, now with a maximum loan of $203,000. The guarantee is insurance against loss from default to the private lender. The VA has assisted nearly three hundred thousand loans to veterans since that time.

This guarantee is free of charge to qualifying veterans. The program includes conventional homes, condominiums, and mobile homes. Because the VA reduces risk to the lender by guaranteeing part of or the entire loan, the lender can safely offer the veteran very low down payments and long terms.

Mortgage Bankers and Brokers

In 1999 there were nearly 350,000 people working in this group, providing financing for real estate. The Mortgage Bankers Association of America (mbaa.org), which represents the mortgage industry, said in May 2003 that it was forecasting a record $3.0 trillion in mortgages written in 2003, beating previous year record-setting mortgage origination by more than half a trillion dollars. The association estimated that approximately $1.95 trillion of that total, or 65 percent, would be due to mortgage refinancing. (For additional information log on to mbaa.org.)

Table 6.2 lists nine occupations in mortgage banking and similar financial operations, and their mean annual salaries for 1999 and 2001.

Personal Credit Institutions

According to the U.S. Department of Labor, 200,550 people worked in 1999 for personal credit institutions, which are establishments primarily engaged in providing loans to individuals. Also included in this industry are establishments primarily engaged in financing retail sales made on the installment plan and financing automobile loans for individuals.

Additional descriptions categorized in this industry include:

- Automobile loans (may include automobile insurance)
- Consumer finance companies
- Financing of automobiles, furniture, appliances, personal airplanes, and so forth, not engaged in deposit banking
- Industrial loan "banks" not engaged in deposit banking
- Industrial loan companies not engaged in deposit banking
- Installment sales finance other than banks

Table 6.2 Mortgage Bankers and Brokers, Selected Business and Financial Operations, Occupations, Mean Annual Salaries for 1999 and 2001

Occupation Title	1999	2001	Annual Percent Change
Management Analysts	$47,060	$53,810	7.6
Accountants and Auditors	38,700	45,940	9.3
Credit Analysts	43,690	45,330	1.7
Budget Analysts	48,820	50,640	1.7
Financial Analysts	59,660	72,410	10.7
Personal Financial Advisors	49,210	56,220	7.6
Financial Examiners	41,850	51,310	11.3
Loan Counselors	39,530	37,750	−2.3
Loan Officers	47,890	53,520	5.9
Total	46,560	50,870	4.6

Source: U.S. Department of Labor, Bureau of Labor Statistics, SIC 616: bls.gov

- Loan companies—small, licensed
- Loan societies—remedial
- Morris plans not engaged in deposit banking
- Mutual benefit associations
- Personal finance companies—small loan, licensed

Business Credit Institutions

According to the U.S. Department of Labor, in 2001 this category employed 147,700 people, compared to 128,800 in 1999, an increase of 14.7 percent. Companies engage in the following business credits:

- Agricultural loan companies
- Automobile finance leasing
- Credit institutions—agricultural
- Farm mortgage companies

- Finance leasing of automobiles, trucks, and machinery
- Finance leasing of equipment and vehicles
- General and industrial loan institutions
- Intermediate investment banks
- Investment companies—small business
- Livestock loan companies
- Loan institutions—general and industrial
- Machinery and equipment finance leasing
- Totalizator equipment finance—leasing and maintenance
- Production credit association—agricultural
- Truck finance leasing

Outlook

Even in the face of economic slowdown, terrorist attacks, and international conflict, the financing of the housing market continues to be resilient. New records have been set in originations, refinancing, and housing starts over the last few years, signaling the American housing system is a strong and functional segment of the economy. The most recent example of this was the Mortgage Bankers Association of America's applications index for home purchases, which hit an all-time record high as of mid-May 2003.

Housing had three consecutive record years. Home sales in 2004 will be somewhat less than in 2003, as we expect a modest increase in mortgage rates. Still, 2004 should be the second-best year ever. The economy continues to improve, consumer confidence is rising, and new jobs should be added, sustaining strong housing demand.

In 2003 there was a record of approximately 6.0 million existing-home sales, up 9.1 percent from the previous year's record of 5.57 million sales. New-home sales in 2003 grew by about 9.7 percent to a record of 1.07 million units. Forecasts for 2004 indicate about 5.75 million existing-home sales and 980,000 new-home sales.

7

SECURITIES AND COMMODITIES BROKERS AND DEALERS

THE U.S. LABOR Department divides securities and commodities into four major categories: securities brokers, dealers, and floating companies; commodities contracts brokers and dealers; securities and commodities exchanges; services allied with the exchanges of securities.

Opportunities

In 2001 these four groups employed 768,070 employees with a mean annual salary of $62,690. Employment in the multi-trillion-dollar financial services and securities industry is expected to continue to grow a little faster than average for all occupations through this decade, as the stock market continues to recover and the economy continues to improve.

In 2001 the United States stock market capitalization was put at $13.98 trillion, down from $15.1 trillion in 1990, but substantially above the $3.1 trillion of 1980. The second-largest stock market capitalization was in Japan at $3.9 trillion in 2001, up from $3.2 trillion in 2000. The third largest was in the United Kingdom with $2.1 trillion in 2001, down from $2.6 trillion in 2000.

Regulatory demands and stiff competition in the marketplace are playing a dramatic role in reshaping the financial services industry and, in particular, the role of the securities dealer. Banking, with its many traditional functions, is no longer the sole province of banks as we know them today. The financial services industry now includes insurance and computer companies, retail merchandise chains, and other firms engaged in managing and protecting other people's money.

Many of the changes taking place in this industry are brought about by the growing sophistication of the consumer and the expansion of high technology and access to information via the Internet. Consumers have been demanding and receiving many new products and services. Liquidity, convenience, level of risk, and the rate of return are all concerns that the consumer must think about, and the complexity of these issues has caused many consumers to seek out the special services available from financial planners.

Families with stock holdings increased sharply from 36.7 percent in 1992 to nearly 50 percent today. The percentage of families holding mutual funds increased to 52 percent in 2001. The percentage of worldwide stock holdings has shifted from Asia to North America, with Europe remaining steady. In 2000 the United States owned over 50 percent of all stocks on these three continents, up from approximately 35 percent in 1990.

Table 7.1 shows eight occupations within the securities and commodities industries and their mean annual salaries for 1999 and 2001.

Table 7.1 Securities Brokers, Dealers, and Floating Companies, Selected Business and Financial Operations, Occupations, Mean Annual Salaries for 1999 and 2001

Occupation Title	*1999*	*2001*	*Annual Percent Change*
Management Analysts	$56,110	$62,950	6.0
Accountants and Auditors	51,800	55,620	3.7
Credit Analysts	52,180	61,510	8.9
Budget Analysts	54,400	64,840	5.1
Personal Financial Advisors	80,420	77,570	−1.8
Financial Examiners	73,010	63,530	−6.5
Loan Counselors	24,660	37,380	25.8
Loan Officers	55,040	68,120	11.9
Total	66,720	69,500	2.1

Source: U.S. Department of Labor, Bureau of Labor Statistics, SIC 651: bls.gov

Securities and Commodities Brokers, Dealers, Exchanges, and Services

The four groups classified by the U.S. Department of Labor show total employment at 768,070 in 2001, a 9.7 percent increase from 700,000 in 1999. The number of securities and commodities dealers increased nearly threefold in the ten years between 1990 and 2000 to 72,900. This segment of the U.S. economy as a share of gross domestic product jumped 341 percent to $144.2 billion from $42.3 billion in 1990.

The biggest increase was among new firms, classified as "other financial investment activity," jumping nearly fivefold in 2001 to 34,800 from 7,100 in 1990. The number of persons employed in this sector also increased sharply to 320,000 workers from 76,000 in 1990. This is a reflection of deregulation, which resulted in consolidations and stronger competitive market.

This consolidation has created one-stop shops for financial services. The consumer can now finance a home; insure health, life, and automobiles; build an investment portfolio; charge consumer goods; and buy and sell real estate through the subsidiaries of a single corporation.

The Securities and Exchange Commission

The U.S. government created the Securities and Exchange Commission (SEC) in 1934 for the protection of the public and of investors against malpractices in the securities and financial markets. The SEC maintains records and makes public all pertinent facts regarding new securities offerings and securities listed on the various exchanges and in over-the-counter markets such as NASDAQ, run by the National Association of Securities Dealers. The SEC also supervises the various stock exchanges. Although the largest is the New York Stock Exchange, generally referred to as "Wall Street" or the "Big Board," others include the American Stock Exchange and several regional exchanges: Midwest, Chicago, Pacific, and Philadelphia.

According to the latest available figures from the U.S. Department of Labor, 5,440 people worked in securities and commodities exchanges, 58,040 worked as securities and commodities brokers and dealers, 17,500 worked as commodities contract brokers and dealers, and 159,010 worked in allied services.

Financial Services Conglomerates

Since 1981 the financial services industry has witnessed the formation of so-called "financial services conglomerates," where one-stop shopping for securities, insurance, banking services, and many other items has become a reality. The rising level of education created a population inclined to seek more sophisticated financial services. Through a variety of acquisitions by national full-line firms, the industry has also witnessed a shrinking network of independent regional firms. Smaller specialty firms have entered the market in surprisingly large numbers, and aggressive steps have been taken by commercial banks and thrift institutions to gain a foothold in the securities business.

In addition to the changing nature of industry participants, several other important changes are occurring. One such change involves the proliferation of innovative products and integrated financial services. Leading the way are such items as asset management accounts, which consolidate all a client's assets into a single account against which checks may be written. Federal deregulation, allowing both banks and securities firms to offer products and services once available only in one location, has resulted in contentious competition. Congressional committees are currently reviewing the entire financial industry to determine whether such competition is ultimately healthy both for the institutions themselves and for the larger economic picture.

One pivotal event that began to change the nature of the securities industry was the acquisition of Bache Halsey Stuart Shields in March 1981 by Prudential Insurance. Prudential's assessment of the marketplace was that the United States would no longer need twenty-five thousand to thirty-five thousand banks, thrift institutions, insurance companies, and securities firms. Instead, the American consumer of financial services would seek a simplification in his or her financial relationships. In Prudential's view, this would result in a growing number of consolidations and a blurring of distinctions among financial institutions.

Demographics have changed over the last twenty to thirty years. Prudential identified the following factors as most critical in its decision to enter the securities industry field in the early eighties:

- Post–World War II baby-boom children were entering their late thirties and early forties.
- Two-income families were becoming the majority.
- Declining mortality rates were creating a substantial increase in the elderly population.
- The effect of inflation on real income and savings of the middle class made the middle-class investor increasingly more sophisticated.
- The advent of computer, video, and other technological developments increased efficiency and reduced the cost of managing information.
- The rapid increase in interest rates resulted in new participants having a significant advantage over existing ones holding low-yielding loan portfolios.
- The integration of the world financial community reshaped the industry.
- Continued urbanization placed a focus on larger metropolitan areas.

The acquisition of Bache by Prudential helped pave the way for other similar acquisitions to occur. Sears, Roebuck and Company, for instance, had for some time been making plans to move beyond its traditional merchandising business into the world of financial services. On the basis of its assessment of the financial environment, Sears decided that it was time to become a primary provider of financial services. During the 1980s, Sears launched its acquisition strategy to become the largest financial service entity and to further blur the distinctions among financial institutions. Thus, Sears acquired the following companies:

- Allstate Insurance Company, one of the nation's largest insurance companies

- Coldwell Banker, the largest independent real estate broker in the United States
- Allstate Savings and Loan, a large California-based thrift institution
- Dean Witter Reynolds, Inc., one of the country's largest securities firms

The New Specialty Firms

The period of financial innovation has given rise to smaller firms as well as huge conglomerates. These are the so-called specialty firms, which identify and carve out a special market niche. One of the most successful of these is the discount firm, which was born in 1975 with the unfixing of commission rates. This particular type of firm functions as an agent, and since it never takes a position, it never acts as a dealer. The specialty firm does not employ sales-people, and it renders no investment advice. Also, to facilitate speed and quality of service, it is very reliant on automated systems to process orders. Some of these firms only trade shares electronically with help of the Internet. Because of its method of operation, the discount firm can offer commission rates one-half to three-quarters below conventional rates charged by full-line commission houses, and on-line brokers can offer commissions as low as $9.99 per trade, regardless of the amount. In the competition for investors' funds, some discount firms now provide money market accounts complete with debit cards and check-writing privileges and even mortgage services. Some of the larger banks have formed partnerships with discount brokerage houses to make such services available to their customers.

Other types of specialty firms are also emerging. These include the tax shelter or "direct participation" firms and the so-called bou-tiques, which have sought other specialties. By concentrating their energies in limited fields of expertise, they are able to compete on the basis of quality of service. Although the upscale customer is usually the target of the specialty firm, these firms will also provide specialized services to a particular market segment, a specific product, or a specific geographical area.

The common threads among the specialty firms are that they conduct business that is limited in scope; they provide personalized service; they are staffed by experts; and because of their size, they are more manageable than their full-service competition.

New Products Explosion

In addition to the diversification that is taking place in the securities industry, a whole new assortment of products has been created to both supplement existing products as well as to satisfy the changing needs of the investor. Part of this explosion of new products has to do with the highly competitive environment in which securities firms operate. But just as important, however, is the fact that consumers of today are more educated and knowledgeable and are seeking more integrated planning and management of their financial affairs.

There is today an almost unlimited number of products from which to choose. These relatively new products include: asset management accounts, money market funds, direct participation programs, standardized equity options, floating rate notes, zero coupon bonds, universal life insurance, real estate securities, precious metals, and electronic brokerage accounts and derivatives.

Electronic brokerage services, also known as online trading, are providing stiff competition for full-service brokers. Through their computers, investors can retrieve analysts' reports and place orders without the help of a broker. At prices as low as $9.99 per trade, electronic trading is one-tenth the cost of its competitors. And, the ease of trading can be done online, without the time-consuming effort of calling the broker.

One of the most attractive, and therefore popular, products of the past decade is the asset management account. It combines the features of a line of credit, a money market account, and the ability to access both assets, and borrowing power through a check or a credit reference.

The money market fund, an integral part of the asset management account, has, on its own, been a major new product development. In 1974 there were only fifteen funds with $1.7 billion in assets. By 1980 assets under management by mutual funds grew to $134.8 billion. A decade later this figure skyrocketed to $1 trillion, and doubled again by 1994 to more than $2 trillion. This product is a popular investment because it is relatively safe, highly liquid, professionally managed, and pays market rates.

The tax shelter or direct participation product has gained popularity as investors look for ways to defer and/or minimize current tax obligations. Financial futures have continued an upward momentum with institutional investors, as the U.S. economy remains volatile. Stock index futures have enabled investors to hedge or trade against overall market movements.

In addition to these new products, older products such as municipal securities and certificates of deposit have generated substantial investor interest.

The municipal bond market received a crushing blow with the October 1987 stock market crash. Large brokerage firms either closed their municipal bond departments or drastically cut back on staffing. Municipal specialists found they had few transferable skills and became the victims of the capricious market. In this instance, however, the slump in municipals resulted primarily from the Tax Reform Act of 1986, which removed several of the bonds' tax-exempt provisions and thus reduced their desirability. Some experts believe the slowdown in municipal bond sales is temporary, citing the continuing need for capital for projects that maintain the country's infrastructure.

The experience of municipal bond specialists is noteworthy for two reasons. First, it points out the inherent unpredictability of the stock market. The market fluctuates according to how the economy, both nationally and globally, is faring; whether people have extra income to invest in stocks; whether corporations are performing well and thus encouraging consumer confidence; or whether international relations are positive. Second, it suggests that successful securities workers and financial planners are those with a broad skills and knowledge base. Specialization is well and good, but in this volatile industry, it often pays to have talents that will be marketable outside your specific field.

The mutual fund industry, however, has grown phenomenally over the last decade, with more than ninety-five hundred mutual funds in mid-2003. A mutual fund is a pool or portfolio of financial assets held by an investment company. Because those assets are diversified, mutual funds tend to track a specific trend and, therefore, may be less volatile than individual securities. For instance, during the Internet boom of the late 1990s, Internet funds did quite well; however, their fortunes diminished with the ensuing crash. Shareholders rely on these investment companies to gain a favorable return on investment from the various holdings, thereby eliminating the need for consumers to operate directly in the market themselves.

From under $300 million in 1980, mutual fund sales grew to more than a trillion dollars during the 1990s.

Investment Banking

A career field closely allied with both the banking and the securities industries is investment banking. This is a high-powered field where competition for positions is fierce and the monetary rewards high. Most of these positions are in the investment banking firms and the major Wall Street brokerage houses, which have investment banking or corporate finance divisions. These large brokerage houses are also referred to as full financial service firms. Investment bankers (or "IBs") are usually hired by companies to conduct capital market transactions, mergers and acquisitions consulting, and other corporate financial services. A well-connected and knowledgeable investment banker will be able to understand a company's needs and can provide investors and strategic partners for its particular situation. IBs usually have lower base salaries, with most of their compensation coming from commissions or fees on the deals they close.

Normally fees charged to companies vary widely in the range of 1 percent to 10 percent of the transaction amount, depending on the size of the transaction and whether there is an equity of debt or a merger consulting fee. IB's bonuses are usually tied to these fees, which sometimes can double or triple the base salary. This is why IB departments are generally the most lucrative for Wall Street firms.

But the price for the high dollar wages sometime takes its toll, as workweeks often exceed sixty hours—and sometimes one hundred hours—when deals have to get completed under time constraints.

Underwriting

Corporate or government underwriting is the traditional activity of the investment banker. However, like other financial industries, investment firms recently have begun offering more financial services. Underwriting means that an investment bank or brokerage firm purchases a new issue of stocks or bonds from a corporation or government body to distribute them in the marketplace.

Investment banking firms work under almost constant pressure to perform, risking vast amounts of capital on a daily basis. Underwriting requires thorough knowledge of the particular industry of the stocks being traded as well as an understanding of the national and international economic scene.

Because of the specialized knowledge required, virtually all members of this profession have a master's degree in business administration or finance as well as experience in several aspects of the investment banking business. Compensation is therefore proportionally higher than it is in other areas.

Mergers and Acquisitions

In response to a sluggish economy and reduced earnings, many major U.S. corporations have discovered that profits can be found in the field of mergers and acquisitions. The stocks of many smaller corporations, as a result of slow earnings, have reduced in value, making their purchase extremely advantageous for those who want to buy enough stock to gain control over the company. Companies have found that buying into an existing company is a less expensive means of diversifying than to develop their own new firm from scratch. In addition, a merger or takeover can stimulate needed capital because the purchase of large blocks of securities drives up the price of the stock, making attempted takeovers lucrative whether or not the final deal occurs. Enter the "corporate raiders," or "white knights" as the case may be, who initiate or foil takeover attempts and rake in tremendous profits in the process.

The investment banking firm serves its corporate client considering a merger or acquisition by conducting a detailed analysis of the company under consideration, including its financial status, management, and operations. The firm advises the client and may be asked to manage the purchase or merger. The company fighting the takeover might also hire an investment banking firm to help maintain its autonomy.

Like corporate underwriters, mergers and acquisitions specialists work long hours and face a tremendous amount of stress. A starting M.B.A. in mergers and acquisitions can earn approximately $50,000 per year, but junior analyst positions available to graduates just out of school are rare.

The Exchanges and Over-the-Counter Market Systems (NASDAQ)

A discussion of the securities industry would be incomplete without a discussion of its heart: the stock exchange and market trading exchanges. Although the largest and best known is the New York Stock Exchange, the American Stock Exchange and the NASDAQ (nasdaq.com) and several regional exchanges exist where stocks are listed and traded. Employment in these exchanges accounts for a relatively small proportion of securities workers, but these positions represent some of the industry's highest salaries.

"Floor" employees conduct direct transactions on the floor of the exchange. These employees must have a seat on the exchange, which is essentially a license that allows them to trade stock. Seats on the New York Stock Exchange are limited and, therefore, expensive. Investment firms own some, but individuals who work only on the exchange hold others. The latter can be divided into two categories: traders and specialists.

Traders trade across the market investing their own capital, and they depend on the fluctuations of the stock prices to make money. Often these traders organize partnerships to diversify their activities. Specialists are traders who have exclusive responsibility for a stock or a group of stocks, ensuring orderly trading and a fair market. The number of specialists is extremely limited because they must have an enormous amount of capital to cover required minimum purchases within their specialty area.

In the over-the market trading systems, the largest is NASDAQ. With more than five thousand stocks, the NASDAQ is an automated quotation system that allows NASDAQ member firms to trade directly among themselves though a complex system of bids (buys) and asks (sells). Rather than an exchange, where all trades are executed through a single firm (the specialist), the NASDAQ market allows for direct trading. In recent years, specialized electronic trading systems, called "ECNs," have boomed on the NASDAQ market (equitystation.com). The onset of the ECN has opened the door to a new breed of trading entrepreneur called the "day trader." These individuals trade for their own account, using personal computers from either their homes or from firms that rent specialized trading space. They trade stocks on volatility and trade to capture a few pennies on each trade. During the bull market of the late 1990s, many day traders who bought long stocks (which means they bought stocks in expectation that they would go up in price) made money. Many of these same players lost big when the collapse of the market wiped out many day traders in 2000. The lessons that were learned were that day trading or "gambling in the market" is better left to the professionals and not inexperienced first-timers.

Income for traders and specialists varies tremendously with the fluctuations of the market. Huge sums can be made and lost in a very short span of time: On average, however, members of the New York Stock Exchange can earn $500,000 or more annually. Traders who trade the over-the-counter markets generally earn base salaries, as well as a portion of what they earn for the trading department. However, the breakneck pace of life on the exchange and the inescapable stress can counteract the benefits of big-time earnings.

Securities Sales Workers and Brokers

Securities sales workers are sometimes referred to as account executives, registered representatives, or, more commonly, as brokers. If an investor wants to either buy or sell securities, he or she goes through the securities sales worker, who relays the order through his or her firm's offices to the floor of a securities exchange. Assuming that securities are not sold or traded on an exchange, the broker sends the order to the firm's trading department, which trades it directly with a dealer in the over-the-counter market.

Securities sales workers rarely do more than just trade on the exchange. Much of what they do depends upon the customer's knowledge of the market. Brokers may have to explain various stock market terms and trading practices, offer counseling of a financial nature, put together an individual's or institution's financial portfolio, and perhaps offer advice on the sale or purchase of individual securities.

Revising a portfolio necessitates knowledge of a variety of investments such as securities, tax shelters, life insurance, mutual funds, or annuities because each investor has particular goals. Some investors, for instance, are looking for long-term investments designed either for capital growth or to provide income over a set number of years. Others might want to place their money in short-term securities that they hope will rise in price very quickly. Securities sales workers also supply the latest price quotations on any securities, as well as information on the financial health and financial activities of corporations that issue securities.

In the beginning, brokers spend much of their time developing and nurturing a clientele. Much of this work is done on the telephone. Once they start, brokers sometimes specialize in one or more types of investments. For instance, brokers who specialize in institutional investing frequently focus on a specific financial product such as stocks, bonds, options, or commodities futures. Some prefer just to work with the sales of new issues such as corporation securities issued to finance the purchase of new equipment or the expansion of an existing plant.

Working Conditions

Most securities sales workers work in offices having computer terminals available that function as "quote machines." These terminals provide ready and continuous access to the prices of various securities. The pace may become fast and even hectic at times, when a lot of buying and selling takes place. Activity also usually increases when a particular measure of economic activity is announced, such as the release of the gross national product, Consumer Price Index, or unemployment rates.

Training and Advancement

In most securities firms, a college education has become the basic requirement for new brokers because they must be well informed about current economic and political events as well as trends. Furthermore, specialized training in finance, business administration, and economics is particularly helpful, although by no means mandatory.

Also, the broker is in essence a salesperson because he or she is promoting the company's financial services. As such, he or she must develop personal qualities to complement the academic credentials.

Securities sales workers must meet the requirements of state licensing boards. These generally include passing a written examination and, in some cases, taking out a personal bond. According to regulations of the securities exchanges where they work or the National Association of Securities Dealers, Inc. (nasdaq.com), sales workers must register as representatives of their firms. Before qualifying as a representative, beginners must pass the Securities and Exchange Commission's General Securities Examination or exams prepared by the exchanges or by NASDAQ. In addition, the larger brokerage firms may require that their brokers pass a second test that permits them to operate nationwide. This latter test is called the Uniform Securities Agents State Law Examination. All of these tests are designed to measure a person's knowledge of the securities business, customer protection, and general bookkeeping methods.

Most sales workers receive on-the-job training that usually lasts about four to six months. Trainees receive classroom schooling in the analysis of securities, effective speaking, and the finer points of salesmanship. But like most fields in which new products are being constantly introduced, brokers periodically take additional courses. Knowledge of the fast-changing world of computers, for instance, requires extra course work and annual training.

Advancement in this field is primarily based on the number and size of the various accounts the broker handles. Those starting out in this field usually handle the accounts of individual investors, while the more experienced workers graduate to the accounts of institutional investors. The latter includes banks, labor unions, corporations, and pension funds. Some brokers eventually progress to the point where they become branch office managers, supervising other employees as well as continuing to handle their accounts. Others are able to advance to even higher-level management positions or become partners in their firms.

Current Employment

By 1994 there were approximately 246,000 securities sales workers, up 23 percent from 1988 and up 214 percent from 1982. In 1999 the sale force registered 189,310 sales workers, who earned an average annual salary of $76,310 and were supplemented by substantially lesser-paid brokerage clerks. By 2001 the sales force increased by 7.9 percent to 204,310, who earned $78,010 annually. The number of brokerage clerks also increased to approximately 67,850, with a mean annual salary of about $35,330.

Employment in this field can be found in all parts of the country and in both small and large firms. However, most securities sales workers are employed by a small number of firms with main offices in large metropolitan areas, most notably in New York City. Employers include national brokerage firms, which have thousands of employees in their nationwide branch offices; regional brokerage firms, which specialize in local corporation interests; discount brokerage houses, which range from very large national firms to small local operations; and investment companies, which perform the same functions as brokerages but specialize in financial planning services.

Job Outlook

The number of securities sales workers is expected to grow only marginally, less than 2 percent annually, with a shift to lower-paid administrative help. This is significantly less than the amazing growth enjoyed by the industry during the 1980s, but securities sales will remain one of the good employment opportunities nationwide. In addition, a substantial number of people in other occupations are involved with selling securities. These include partners and branch office managers in securities firms as well as insurance agents and brokers offering securities to their customers.

Transferees and those who change careers or leave the labor force will create most new positions. Because it is so hard to establish and maintain a good clientele, the dropout rate among beginners is quite high. However, because earnings are good and training is extensive, the potential for success is considerable.

Overall Outlook for the Securities Industry

Employment in the securities industry grew from 700,080 in 1999 to 768,700 in 2001, an increase of 9.1 percent. With the economy recovering we can foresee rising personal incomes and an increase in the funds available for investments. More individual consumers are expected to seek advice from securities sales representatives regarding the broad range of investment alternatives, resulting in increased purchases of common stocks, mutual funds, and other financial products. Deregulation has enabled brokers to offer checking and savings options, insurance products such as annuities and life insurance, and certificates of deposit.

Institutional investments will grow as more people enroll in pension plans, set up individual retirement accounts, establish trust funds, and contribute to colleges and other nonprofit institutions. In addition, more representatives will be needed to sell securities issued by new and expanding corporations and by state and local governments financing public improvements.

Earnings

According to the Securities Industry Association, earnings in this field vary widely. Median annual earnings were $37,300 in 1994.

This increased to $46,545 in 2001, with beginning securities sales workers earning on average $30,000 annually, according to Bureau of Labor Statistics figures. Full-time, experienced securities sales workers who handle the accounts of individual investors earn between $70,000 and $100,000, according to an industry survey, while those who handle the accounts of institutional investors (i.e., organizations) average 150 percent more, or about $240,000.

Trainees are usually paid a salary until they meet licensing and registration requirements. Even after requirements are fulfilled, some companies continue to pay their brokers a salary until the brokers' commissions increase to a certain level.

As you can see from Table 7.2, this industry pays considerably more than all other financial intermediaries. The salaries of people working in business and financial operations were 13.7 percent higher than the average of all. Part of this is due to the concentration of the industry in the New York area, but a substantial part is also due to risk taking. For the most part, earnings depend upon commissions. When the market is active, earnings will be high, and vice versa. At times many firms provide their brokers with income by allowing them to draw some salary based on potential commissions. This helps insulate brokers from the ups and downs of the marketplace.

Research

All major brokerage firms and investment banking firms, as well as many banks and corporations, employ securities analysts or stock analysts whose job consists of studying stocks and bonds, usually within a specific industry. They issue regular reports assessing the value of these securities and predicting their growth potential in view of current economic trends.

Table 7.2 Services Allied with the Exchanges of Securities, Selected Business and Financial Operations, Occupations, Mean Annual Salary for 1999 and 2001

Occupation Title	1999	2001	Annual Percent Change
Management Analysts	$58,070	$66,460	7.2
Accountants and Auditors	52,030	55,220	3.1
Credit Analysts	67,600	60,310	−5.4
Budget Analysts	55,630	69,110	12.1
Financial Analysts	72,290	83,030	7.4
Personal Financial Advisors	67,220	73,250	4.5
Financial Examiners	87,070	86,820	−0.2
Loan Counselors	NA	31,320	NA
Loan Officers	52,720	53,220	0.4
Total	67,750	70,300	1.9

Source: U.S. Department of Labor, Bureau of Labor Statistics, SIC 628—Commercial Banks: bls.gov

Stock analysts generally receive on-the-job training, but increasingly graduate degrees are becoming the norm. The Association for Investment Management and research provides further training and grants the prestigious Chartered Financial Analyst (CFA) designation. Entry-level research assistants receive $35,000, while experienced analysts earn between $50,000 and $63,000. Department heads or senior analysts enjoy base salaries of more than $100,000.

Operational and market analysts in securities and commodities earn the highest salaries; insurance carriers earn the lowest. There are about twenty-seven thousand operational and market analysts employed by the industry. Operational research analysts average $53,432 in annual wages, and market analysts average $47,820. In addition there are 1,170 economists who earn average annual salaries of $82,950 and 2,040 statisticians who earn $54,555.

Table 7.3 compares wages across financial intermediaries.

Table 7.3 Annual 2001 Wage Comparison, Financial Intermediaries

	Mean Annual Wage	Finance-Business	Computers	Sales Admin. Support
Depository Institutions	$49,970	$57,630	$44,880	$24,740
Nondepository Institutions	49,350	57,750	45,220	28,650
Central Reserve	54,070	61,330	57,480	29,190
Mortgage Bankers	50,870	54,930	48,580	30,090
Securities/ Commodities Dealers	69,740	66,210	76,310	33,530
Average, first four institutions	51,065	57,910	49,040	28,168
Securities/ Commodities to five others	+13.7%	+12.4%	+15.6%	+14.9%

Source: U.S. Department of Labor, SIC 60, 61, 601, and 616: bls.gov

8

INSURANCE COMPANIES AND REAL ESTATE

INSURANCE IS A device for reducing some of the risks inherent in the economy and providing some degree of certainty. In addition to contributing to the economy by preserving human life values and protecting against the financial consequences of their loss, insurance also adds to both the financing business industry and government. Expanding production is needed to maintain economic growth, to fuel employment, and to develop a balanced economy. Insurance helps stabilize the economy by reducing risk and by financing businesses as well as individuals.

Opportunities

The total number of employees in the insurance sector increased by 10.8 percent between 1990 and 2001, with insurance carriers up 9.2 percent and agents, brokers, and services by 14.5 percent. There was a shift in the number of establishments created away from carriers to agents. While the total number of establishments increased 23.3 percent, the number of carriers dropped 13.6 percent and the number of agents increased 37.6 percent. This is not unusual as there was a consolidation of most U.S. companies during this period, and insurance was not any different. The gross domestic product contribution of insurance companies jumped dramatically by 459 percent over this span of time, reflecting the sharp increases in need of protection against law suits.

Yahoo lists 1,160 individual insurance companies and sources on the Web. Of these, 359 are life insurance, 10 are title insurance, 113 are brokerage, and 195 are auto insurance. Some of the sources listed below provide free quotes:

- Homeowners Insurance Quotes Online offers free home owners insurance quotes and rates from multiple companies: homeownerswiz.com.
- American Home Shield (AHS), providers of car and home insurance, offers online quotes: americanhomeshield.com.
- Homeowners Insurance Quotes, Inc. offers mortgage and home owners insurance quotes: homeowners-insurance-quotes-inc.com.

Insurance companies are divided into various groups. The major ones are: auto, home, life, accident, health, business, fire, marine, flood, casualty, property title, and renter insurance. Two major parts of the insurance business are social and voluntary. Social insurance is federal and state insurance, such as employment security, social security, old age, and survivors insurance. Voluntary insurance covers just about anything from fire to gambling.

Table 8.1 lists employment and salary statistics for different parts of the insurance industry.

All Risks Are Insurable

It has been said, "As a matter of theory, all risk is insurable." This is true, as long as the risk lends itself to a reasonable calculation based on a large number of observations. Insurance today is based on a long experience of observations and generally is a very stable and profitable business. The industry is so vast that an inquiry on a website about U.S. insurance produced nearly two million items. As long as we keep hurting or suing each other, the insurance sec-

Table 8.1 Insurance Companies, Number of Employees, and Mean Annual Wage, 2001

Type	Employment	Mean Annual Wage
Insurance Carriers (SIC 63)	1,474,580	$42,630
Insurance Agents (SIC 64)	758,730	39,940
Life Insurance (SIC 631)	379,460	43,790
Management Occupations	39,810	82,020
Chief Executives	3,550	121,170
Accident/Health and Medical (SIC 632)	367,080	39,780
Management Occupations	33,400	78,440
Chief Executives	2,430	127,790
Fire, Marine, Casualty (SIC 633)	562,870	44,460
Management Occupations	38,430	81,030
Chief Executives	2,610	120,080
Surety Insurance (SIC 635)	21,710	50,150
Management Occupations	2,900	92,720
Chief Executives	370	119,920
Title Insurance (SIC 636)	83,970	38,200
Management Occupations	9,920	71,850
Chief Executives	1,200	103,100
Pension, Health, Welfare (SIC 637)	56,220	38,970
Management Occupations	6,240	80,970
Chief Executives	900	112,770
Total (SIC 63 and SIC 64)	2,233,310	41,285

Source: U.S. Department of Labor: bls.gov

tor will prosper. In the year 2000 we had 6,394,000 motor vehicle accidents that resulted in 41,800 deaths and 3,189,000 injuries; 512 deaths and 104,424 railroad injuries; 701 deaths and 4,355 injuries in recreational boating; and 595 deaths in general aviation. In addition, we had 1,606,000 violent crimes, 15,500 murders, and 1.1 million stolen vehicles.

It's interesting to note in an FBI report issued in mid-June 2003 that the top ten cities with major crimes had populations of more than five hundred thousand, and seven of these cities are located in the East. Washington, D.C., is ranked number one—called by some the U.S. Murder Capital—leading with 45.8 homicides per capita, beating Detroit with 42.0. Phoenix was the last on the list, with 12.9 homicides per capita. Even a historically notorious high-crime area like Chicago had a per capita murder rate less than half that of Washington D.C. (22.3). One can reasonably ask: Where are the Chicago mobsters? Apparently in Washington, D.C.

In 1983 we had 612,000 lawyers and only 98,000 economists, who were trying with various degrees of success to advise business and government on how to run a business and the country. (The number of lawyers was nearly twice that of financial managers.) In 2001, eighteen years later, the number of lawyers increased to 929,000, a jump of 52 percent, while the number of economists grew to 135,000, an increase of 37.7 percent. In 2001, legal services employed a total of 1,026,000 people, an 11.4 percent increase in one year! There were 177,000 legal services establishments with a payroll of $62 billion, up 8.8 percent in one year. Senator Trent Lott characterized trial lawyers as a "pack of wolves who are going to kill the goose that laid the golden egg" if they are not reined in.

At the end of June 2003, lawyers in Boston called what they described as the Obesity Lawsuit Conference with public officials to plan how to sue fast-food chains for obesity. This came a day after House Judiciary Committee member Representative Ric Keller, a Florida Republican, introduced a bill titled the "Personal Responsibility in Food Consumption Act," which was aimed in protecting food companies from "frivolous lawsuits."

Lawsuits from 1975 through 2001 cost U.S. citizens $2.8 trillion. To put it in perspective, this is 25.3 percent of the 2003 GDP, or $11.06 trillion of all goods and services produced in 2003.

Frivolous lawsuits have slapped outrageous penalties on the U.S. economy and increased the amount of insurance protection required by business and the general public. Much of this will not change soon; so insurance companies will continue to grow.

Real Estate

Of the total of about 1.6 million workers in real estate in 2002, 38 percent were working as real estate operators (SIC 651), 51 percent as real estate agents and managers (SIC 653), 3 percent as title abstract officers (SIC 654), and 8 percent as land developers (SIC 655).

A real estate lending officer accepts applications for real estate loans and guides loan applications through an approval committee; collects and analyzes financial data; and arranges to have property appraised and for deeds and other legal documents to be made ready. Banks also employ about five thousand real estate appraisers and assessors, whose average pay was $56,910 in 2001, compared to $50,050 in 1999.

Real Estate Outlook

Low rates are pushing home refinancing to a new high. Housing has traditionally followed the path of interest rates, collapsing during the times of high rates and improving with mortgage rates declining. The National Association of Home Builders forecast 1.07 million new home sales in 2003 and 1.96 million housing starts. As long as low interest rates are available, housing will do very well, possibly through the first nine months of 2004.

Low interest rates help housing and stimulate economic growth. This was borne out in the improvement of overall economic performance in the second half of 2003. This indicates that a year from the summer of 2003, the Fed may well begin to tighten the economic reins and housing will begin to slow down. Low interest rates over the last forty-five years have helped housing tremendously, increasing the home-ownership rate to an all-time record of 67.9 percent, according to the U.S. Census Bureau. This resulted in a 26 percent increase in the past eight years in the price of the median single-family home from $110,500 in 1995 to $170,000 in 2003. This increase pushed nearly fourteen million families to pay over 30 percent of their income for housing.

The situation is quite different in commercial real estate, where the office situation in particular has deteriorated since mid-2000. The national office vacancy rate in mid-2000 was 8.6 percent, and in the first quarter of 2003 it increased sharply to 16.9 percent. In three major cities the vacancy rate is now over 20 percent, with Austin at 25.7 percent (in December 2000 it was 5.0 percent), Atlanta at 22.3 percent (9.9 percent in 2000), and Denver at 21.0 percent (9 percent in 2000). This situation threatens to impair the future performance of banks' commercial real estate loan portfolios. Commercial banks' delinquent loans declined sharply from 8 percent in 1991 to just under 2 percent in late 1991, but it has started to edge up slightly since then. Charge-off increased from a low of $38 million in 1997 to $1.17 billion in 2002.

It's clear that in 2004, 2005, and 2006 we will experience fall-out in housing starts and sales and moderation in prices, something to consider when looking for a job in this field. We will also see further increases in commercial vacancies, not only in office buildings, but also in the manufacturing sector. For a detailed discussion, see the June 23, 2003, FDIC article, "How Long Can Bank Portfolios Withstand Problems in Commercial Real Estate?" (fdic.gov).

Table 8.2 lists five occupational divisions within real estate and their mean annual wages for 1999.

Table 8.2 Real Estate Number of Employees and Mean Annual Wage, 1999

Type	Employment	Mean Annual Wage
Real Estate Operators (SIC 651)	576,090	$26,250
Management Occupations	75,440	47,590
Chief Executives	3,620	94,160
Real Estate Agents and Managers (SIC 653)	754,810	31,860
Management Occupations	126,110	54,090
Chief Executives	5,940	109,200
Title Abstract Offices (SIC 654)	43,050	32,380
Management Occupations	4,840	61,090
Chief Executives	850	83,090
Land Developers (SIC 655)	123,390	32,720
Management Occupations	18,710	65,200
Chief Executives	1,500	100,260
Total Real Estate (SIC 65)	1,497,340	29,790
Management Occupations	225,090	52,990
Chief Executives	11,910	101,640

Source: U.S. Department of Labor, SIC 65: bls.gov

9

CAREERS IN FINANCIAL SERVICES

IN THIS CHAPTER we will examine more closely the opportunities available in financial services management operations, business and financial operations, office and administrative support, and computers and mathematical operations.

Opportunities in Management Operations

Most financial institutions have a president who directs and oversees the operations of the institution; several vice presidents who are really general managers and are in control of specific bank departments; and a comptroller or cashier who, unlike a cashier in a department store, is an executive officer responsible for bank property. In 2001, the mean annual wage of a chief executive at a commercial bank was $115,110, a 7.0 percent increase since 1999. Annual pay for all managers in 2001 was $75,490, up 4.2 percent from 1999. The annual wage in all depository institutions was $112,640, up from $74,010. In 2001, there were 149,600 managers in commercial banks, up from 146,360 in 1999. In all depository institutions there were 266,350 managers. Even larger banks may need a treasurer or other senior staffers to supervise specific sections within a bank's different departments. Some smaller banks (especially those located in small communities) may not need so many senior officers. Managerial occupations dropped from 758,628 in 1999 to 529,260 in 2001. This clearly indicates the technological change throughout the industry and the movement toward greater efficiency, which, by the way, is true of all financial intermediaries.

Job Outlook

The employment of bank officers and managers is expected to increase slightly despite the enormous attempt to cut costs. Rising costs due to expanded bank services will most likely require more officers to provide better and expanded management techniques. As the world becomes more economically interdependent, international trade and investment will be greatly facilitated by expanded international banking activities. Growth areas within the banking industry include financial services and acquisitions and mergers. Competition for the available managerial positions in banking, which has always been tough, will probably stiffen as the number of qualified applicants increases.

Salaries for bank officers have become more differentiated in the industry, with professional specialty assuming a greater role in salary determination. Variables such as size and type of institution, geographic location, and an individual's experience and educational background affect earnings as well. Salaries tend to be higher in major metropolitan areas, and surveys show that banks in the Northeast pay higher salaries than their counterparts elsewhere in the country. Education plays a significant role in starting salaries, with master's degree holders earning more than those with bachelor's degrees. Those with a master's in business administration are most in demand and, therefore, are able to command even higher salaries.

Opportunities in Business and Financial Operations

Overall, salaries for bank managers are the highest at $75,490; credit unions pay the lowest. Many bank officers in business and financial operations, especially those in commercial banks, receive annual bonuses ranging from 6 percent of the base salary for an officer trainee with a bachelor's degree at a small bank to 30 percent or more for the chief executive officer of a large bank. Although salaries in the banking industry may not reach the levels in other professions, bankers enjoy excellent benefits and a high degree of job security. Unlike other industries, banks tend to maintain employment levels regardless of economic fluctuations.

Banks have greatly expanded the type and number of financial services they now offer. Because of this, bank officers are usually required to have a rudimentary knowledge of allied fields such as insurance, real estate, securities, or agriculture. They must also have a broad knowledge of business activities, so they can relate to the operations of the bank's different departments. Thus, a wide variety of careers are available to workers who want to specialize within the banking profession.

Consumer banking is often referred to as retail banking and involves many bank services to individual customers. These services include checking and savings accounts, single-payment and installment loans, bank credit cards, and traveler's checks.

You may want to specialize in personal, installment, commercial, real estate, or agricultural loans. Or you may like to become a loan officer who handles several types of loans, thereby increasing your flexibility. For personal loan applications, an individual's credit and collateral must be properly evaluated. In the case of a business loan, the loan officer must be able to analyze a company's financial position or strength as well as be familiar with business activities and the direction of the economy. Business loan officers should be familiar with commercial law, banking regulations, merchandising and production practices, and economics.

Loan Officers

Loan officers provide loan services to businesses and other organizations by analyzing financial data, inspecting businesses, conducting credit investigations, and arranging for the preparation of loan notes and other legal documents. One-third of the financial positions are among lending officers who have salaries of $50,000 or more.

Financial Analysts and Personal Financial Advisors

We will discuss the two categories of financial analysts and personal financial advisors together since their duties and responsibilities are similar.

Personal financial advisors accept applications for personal loans and bank credit cards; interview loan applicants; collect and analyze financial data; steer loan applications through the committee that must approve the loans; and set up repayment schedules, among other duties.

Financial analysts help individuals set up investment portfolios by describing a wide variety of available investments. Bank officers in trust management require knowledge of financial planning and investment sources for estate and trust administration. The investment income from these accounts is vitally important because it may help support families, send people to college, or start a retirement pension.

The burgeoning of investment opportunities coupled with confusing tax laws has given rise to a need for more personal financial planners, people who understand both investments and the tax advantages to be gained through wise distribution of assets. The complexity of the task has led to increasing sophistication in a field that formerly has been dominated by private individuals who styled themselves financial planners but had no formal training. Now financial planners are often certified through programs offered at several universities and through financial planning organizations with educational programs.

Nature of the Work

A financial planner can be self-employed or found as an employee in a bank, an accounting firm, an insurance company, a financial planning firm, or a brokerage firm. He or she is someone who assists both individuals and businesses in utilizing their financial resources to achieve certain objectives. The resources used could be income, savings, or money made from previous investments.

Financial planners are involved with wealth management, estate planning, tax planning, and retirement planning. They must integrate all the facets of a client's finances into a comprehensive plan that meets the client's goals and objectives.

Though the occupations related to financial planning fall to a certain extent under categories previously described in this book, we have intentionally separated this field because it is a relatively new profession.

Working Conditions

While most financial planners work for financial institutions, some are self-employed consultants who provide financial plans for a set fee. The fee can either be a certain percentage of the client's total assets or be determined on an hourly basis, or both. Other financial planners may work for a financial institution, such as a bank, securities firm, or an insurance company. Those working for other companies are usually paid on the basis of commissions. Products on which they earn commissions may include such items as real estate, trust services, insurance, securities, and individual retirement accounts. The latter is "commission-only" compensation. Most planners rely on a combination of set fees and commissions.

Like certain bank employees and securities sales workers, those involved in financial planning are constantly in contact with the public. They must, therefore, present a businesslike image to clients. Most of these professionals work in offices.

Training and Advancement

Most financial planners have at least a four-year college degree. To be best prepared for this field, the International Association of Financial Planning, a trade group based in Atlanta, Georgia, recommends taking courses in accounting, finance, economics, marketing, general business, business law, small business management, mathematics, human behavior counseling, investments, taxes, estate planning, and computer science.

Many universities offer programs directed toward the financial planning field, usually with majors in business. Many financial planners who want to advance in their field seek professional designations such as Certified Financial Planner (CFP) and/or Chartered Financial Consultant (ChFC).

Two organizations within the profession, the International Association for Financial Planning and the Institute of Certified Financial Planners, have established strict requirements for those who would be certified as financial planners. A more sophisticated consumer public is likely to seek out planners who have these credentials. Most states have some requirements for investment advisors, which include financial planners. Investment advisors must generally be registered federally under the Investment Advisor Act of 1940.

Obtaining these designations requires successfully completing six to ten college-level courses, which are often available through correspondence study. In addition to these educational requirements, the individual must have spent at least one year dealing with financial clients.

Earnings

Income among financial planners varies much like that of securities sales workers. The income may be high if the client's financial goals are complex. "Fee only" financial planners charge set fees for preparing financial plans. This amount can be as low as $500 and as much as $30,000. "Commission only" planners do not charge for preparing specific plans but instead receive commissions, the size of which depends mostly on the purchase of securities and other financial products. As already mentioned, most planners use a combination of fees and commissions. Annual earnings for financial planners range from $44,840 to $80,450.

Credit Analysts

Credit analysts study financial statements and other credit data to evaluate a company's financial strength and ability to make payments on a loan, and prepare reports from which loan officers determine credit risks.

Other Occupations

Among the business and financial occupations there are also the following positions:

- Compliance officers with 10,880 workers
- Management analysts with 23,100 workers
- Budget analysts with 2,900 workers
- Financial examiners with 9,590 workers

Most of these occupations require a similar background of education and experience.

Working Conditions

Customers' impressions of both the surroundings and the employees of a financial institution play a role in that institution's success. Consequently, officers and managers of a bank are usually provided with attractive, comfortable offices and are frequently required to dress in conservative attire. Bank officers and managers are typically required to work a forty-hour week, although establishing and maintaining business contacts usually requires time spent on the job beyond forty hours. Civic functions and other community developments also may result in overtime work.

Training and Advancement

Individuals who have successfully completed a management trainee program, or clerks or tellers who have demonstrated an aptitude for management-level positions typically fill bank officer and management slots. A college education is usually required before one is allowed into a management trainee program. The degrees that serve as good preparation for officer training programs are those in business administration, with a major in finance, or a liberal arts program that includes courses in accounting, economics, statistics, commercial law, and computers. Those with an even stronger educational background, particularly a master's in business administration (M.B.A.), have an advantage over others. However, banks do hire people with diverse backgrounds to meet the needs of the great variety of businesses and industries they must deal with in the regular course of business. Individuals interested in becoming bank officers and managers must possess an ability to analyze detailed information, to work independently, and to counsel and otherwise deal directly with clients.

Small banks have the fewest number of positions available, and advancement to officer or management positions may come more slowly. Promotions may come more quickly or are, at best, more accessible in large banks, where there are more special training programs. For senior-level programs, however, an individual usually is required to have several years of work experience in addition to the appropriate educational requirements.

For promotional opportunities, education, experience, and ability are stressed in most professional and nonprofessional fields. Banks often provide opportunities for their workers to advance through special study courses. Banking associations in particular sponsor any training programs, some of which are held in conjunction with local universities.

Opportunities in Office and Administrative Support

This is the largest sector of employees among financial intermediaries, employing more than three million workers. Salaries earned are the lowest in this sector, but it is a good place to start a career. Employment of office and administrative support in financial institutions has enjoyed phenomenal annual growth of 11.7 percent since 1999.

Bank Tellers

The individual with whom the bank customer generally deals most often is the bank teller, the person "out front" who cashes checks, receives deposits, and makes withdrawals. Smaller banks usually have just one and sometimes two all-purpose tellers, while large banks may have their tellers specializing in different functions. For instance, one teller may do nothing but keep records and do the paperwork for customer loans; another may only accept payment for a customer's utility bills; while yet others might process a variety of money market accounts, certificates of deposit, and foreign currencies exchanges.

The most common teller is the commercial teller, who primarily cashes checks and handles deposits and withdrawals from checking and savings accounts and might service or "replenish" ATMs. It is this type of teller that most of us, as bank customers, come in contact with.

A teller's day usually begins before the actual start of banking hours and frequently continues after the close of business. The typical day begins with receiving and counting money for the cash drawer, which will then be used for payments during the day. After regular banking hours, tellers must count the cash they have in their drawers, list the currency received on a settlement sheet, and balance the day's account. This is a straightforward assignment, but one that requires a great deal of attention to detail and a certain aptitude with numbers.

Training and Advancement

Good clerical skills are also necessary requirements for a teller. Although not required by all banks, possession of a high school diploma is considered the basic background requirement at most institutions.

New tellers are asked to observe more experienced tellers for several days before being permitted to do the job. Beginners usually start out as commercial tellers, where training is completed in about three to four weeks. Specialized tellers usually require a greater amount of work experience.

Experienced tellers sometimes advance to head teller in a bank or to a position as customer service representative. To be promoted from teller to bank officer or loan officer or to some managerial position requires not only work experience but frequently also advanced course work at a university, specialized training, or both.

Banks tend to promote from within, and tellers can prepare for advancement in a number of ways. First, they can obtain, if they have not already done so, a college degree. Second, they can take courses accredited by the American Institute of Banking (AIB) (aba.com/Conferences+and+Education/aib_main.htm), the Bank Administration Institute (BAI) (bai.org), and the Institute of Consumer Financial Education (ICFE) (icfe.info). AIB has more than 450 chapters in the United States. These institutes help banks to conduct training programs, while some banks have established their own teller-certification training programs.

Current Employment

Commercial bank tellers held about 559,000 jobs in 1994. This number declined sharply to only 355,810 in 2001, due to modernization and a general improvement in the way we handle money.

The overwhelming majority of bank tellers work in depository institutions, with commercial banks, savings institutions, and credit unions employing 97 percent of all tellers. Approximately 75 percent of all tellers work full-time.

Because of the growing use of automatic teller machines (ATMs) and other electronic equipment and the assumption of some banking functions by other financial institutions, the Bureau of Labor Statistics estimates a moderate decrease of about 4 percent in the number of bank tellers employed in all industries by 2005. The majority of employment opportunities in this field will be created not by new openings but by replacement needs. Because of increased competition for available jobs, education will become a more significant factor in hiring.

Qualities and Skills

Bank tellers require the following personal attributes in order to be successful:

- Businesslike appearance
- Interpersonal skills
- Good business judgment
- Clerical skills
- Accuracy and attention to detail
- Honesty
- Money-handling ability
- Communications skills

Experience

A high school education, with math and clerical courses, is the minimum requirement. A college education stressing business and liberal arts courses, continuing (on-the-job) training, and experience in a similar job are also very useful for advancement.

Computer Technology in the Financial Industry

The rise in banking productivity that started in the 1960s and is still continuing owes a lot to advances made in computer technology and its application throughout the banking industry.

The computer has had its greatest impact on check handling. Its full potential is only now being realized. For loan operations, for instance, electronic data processing (EDP) has been used for information retrieval as well as in administration and bookkeeping operations of loan categories such as installment loans. Major beneficiaries of computer applications have been mortgage servicing, bank credit card billing, credit information, and accounting. The proportion of people in installment loan operations has declined with the onset of the computer, but staff working in other areas, such as handling bank credit cards, has grown in recent years. Business loan operations have remained relatively labor intensive because of their specialized nature and need for maintaining close customer relations. However, even here the computer's role is becoming increasingly important. The computer provides current credit analysis and serves as an indicator of whether the loan applicant is bankrupt. For larger banks with international operations, the computer makes credit information readily available so that decisions can be made more quickly.

Computer technology has also helped to improve productivity in trust departments. Here it has been applied to information retrieval for purposes of controlling individual accounts as well as for use in stock trading.

Potentially, the most important use of the computer for the banking industry remains electronic funds transfer (EFT). This technology has been around for nearly thirty years, although it has been used in a great capacity only since the 1970s. The further use of EFT in the coming years will be facilitated by its cost advantage over conventional methods and the growing competition among financial institutions.

Computer technology has enabled the banking industry to expand globally, even at the consumer level. Automatic teller machines are capable of instant international transfer of funds. Travelers are advised to use their personal credit or ATM cards at ATMs throughout Europe to get more advantageous currency exchange rates (typically the interbank rate), obtaining funds directly from their U.S. accounts rather than through the foreign banks.

With the spread of EFT and other computerized and automated transactions, knowledge of computer operations has become a must for most bank employees in managerial positions.

The spread of computers has also changed the number and mix of employment opportunities available at banks. As mentioned above, the proliferation of ATMs and computer banking are reducing the number of tellers. Since computers perform more and more of the bank's clerical tasks, clerical workers, in many cases, no longer deal directly with information.

Job opportunities in electronic data processing, especially as it is applied to banking, should continue to be good. It is a relatively new field with broad usefulness and rapid technological growth. It is a fair prediction that computers will control more and more of a bank's functions in the future.

This development has led to the need for more computer operators, programmers, and analysts in banks. Operators simply operate the computers, programmers write the instructions that tell the computer what to do with the information it receives, and a systems analyst analyzes the computer needs of the company and determines what sort of system is needed.

In 1994, of all employees in the banking industry, 26,344 were computer scientists and related workers, 21,032 were systems analysts, and 5,309 were computer programmers or programmer aids. Nationwide, computer systems analysis is projected to be among the fastest-growing occupations, according to the Bureau of Labor Statistics. By 2005, the number of computer scientists and related workers in banking is expected to increase to 46,000, with systems analysts growing to 36,000. In the financial services industry, an additional 70,000 jobs for computer systems analysts are expected, showing a growth of over 80 percent.

Career Development

The banking profession is one that encourages both personal and professional development. Several organizations exist to provide training at all levels of experience and within virtually any specialty area of banking. Many banks offer their own advanced training programs, as do several of the large colleges offering business and finance degrees. With additional education come increased salaries and opportunities for promotion. Two organizations sponsoring widely recognized and attended seminars on banking include the American Bankers Association (ABA) and the American Institute of Banking (AIB). Appendix B lists colleges and universities offering degrees in finance and banking.

American Bankers Association

The most extensive national program for bank officers is offered through the American Bankers Association (aba.com). Each of the ABA's twelve schools deals with a different phase of banking. Participants attend annual sessions on subjects such as installment credit, international banking, and commercial lending. The ABA also sponsors seminars and conferences and provides textbooks and other educational materials. ABA provides the following courses: Agricultural and Rural Credit, Business Banking, Communications Tools, Community Bank Tax, Community Banking, Compliance, Consumer Education, Corporate Governance, Financial Fraud, Human Resources, ICB Certification, Insurance, International, Marketing, Privacy, Real Estate, Retail Banking, Securities, Supplier Directory, Technology Payments, Trust. For junior bank staff, the American Institute of Banking fills the same educational need.

American Institute of Banking

The American Institute of Banking (aba.com/conferences+and+ education/aib_main.htm) is the educational arm of the ABA and offers a wide variety of courses ranging from basic skills seminars to graduate-level courses and seminars in finance and economics for bank officers. The organization offers training in retail banking, processing, and distribution. AIB courses are open to members of the ABA only. It educates more than 150,000 bankers every year, not including those taking shorter seminar programs (an additional 75,000 to 100,000 bankers).

AIB courses are of two basic types: textbook-based and seminar (or forum) courses. The first is similar to a regular classroom course, with lectures and examinations. The second type is more informal, with discussion leaders guiding the group to offer greater opportunity for student participation. The seminar is used for more advanced subjects. Topics for the courses range from the general (such as principles of accounting) to the specific (bank credit cards). The main subject areas are: accounting, economics, marketing, investment and finance, data processing, business administration, political science, law, speech, English, and psychology.

The institute awards certificates to students who have completed a certain number of the courses offered. There are four different levels: basic, standard, advanced, and general. To earn a certificate in any of the first three, a student must satisfactorily complete a specific number of credit courses in the following four areas of study:

- Foundations of banking
- Banking functions
- Management and supervision
- Language and communication

In addition, the operations of banks have been greatly changed by the expanded use of the computer and other data processing equipment. Knowledge of this equipment and its application is important to upgrade one's managerial skills and advancement opportunities.

10

CORPORATE AND
INDUSTRIAL FINANCE

ALTHOUGH MOST INDIVIDUALS interested in financial careers will work in financial organizations such as banks, savings and loan associations, brokerage firms, and financial planning companies, career opportunities are plentiful within the corporate and industrial complex. Virtually every firm—whether in manufacturing, communications, education, health care, real estate, or finance—has one or more financial managers or financial analysts who prepare the financial reports that enable the firm to conduct its operations and satisfy tax and regulatory requirements. These functions vary depending on the specific job description, but they are often closely related to both securities and investment planning and accounting functions.

The financial staff in corporate and industrial finance analyzes and interprets data particular to that industry and makes recommendations to management staff for decision making. The finan-

115

cial staff in a manufacturing firm might oversee the company's cash and liquid assets; raise funds in capital markets; project costs, changes in technology, needs for investment capital, and market demand for the manufactured commodity; and determine price structures for manufactured goods. All long-range planning necessarily involves the work of financial analysts, managers, and planners.

Financial Managers

Often called the treasurer or controller, the financial manager must maintain a constant appraisal of the firm's present and future financial status. In small firms, the controller's duties include all financial management functions, and in large firms, the treasurer or chief financial officer oversees all financial management departments and helps top managers develop financial and economic policy.

Nature of the Work

The reports generated by the financial management department include income statements, balance sheets, and depreciation schedules. Controllers oversee the accounting, audit, or budget departments. Cash managers control the flow of cash receipts and disbursements. Risk and insurance managers oversee programs to minimize risks and losses that may arise from financial transactions and business operations. Credit card operations managers establish credit rating criteria, determine credit limits, and monitor their institution's extension of credit. Reserve officers review the corporation's financial statements and direct the purchase and sale of bonds and other securities to maintain the asset-liability ratio required by law.

Training and Advancement

A bachelor's degree in accounting, finance, or business administration (with an emphasis on accounting or finance) is the typical background for most entry-level financial managers. A master's degree will usually ensure higher starting salaries as well as more rapid advancement. Promoting experienced, technically skilled professional personnel from the ranks of accountants, budget analysts, credit analysts, loan officers, or securities analysts fills many financial management positions. Promotions occur more rapidly in large firms than in small companies, where the number of available positions is limited.

Experience, ability, and leadership are the qualities emphasized for advancement, but promotion may be accelerated through continuing education. Firms often provide opportunities for special study through local colleges and universities. Special schools connected with financial management and banking associations offer seminars throughout the country. Each program deals with a specific phase of financial management: accounting management, budget management, corporate cash management, financial analysis, international finance, and data processing systems procedures and management.

Potential financial managers need to be able to work independently and analyze detailed information, communicate clearly both orally and in writing, and establish effective interpersonal relationships with professional staff members under their supervision. Knowledge of computers and data processing programs is a prerequisite and is vital for enhancing advancement opportunities. Because this skills base is critical for efficient business operation, experienced financial managers may transfer to similar positions in other industries.

The salary level varies according to the size and location of the organization, with higher salaries paid in large institutions and major metropolitan areas. Financial managers in private industry often receive additional compensation in the form of bonuses, which also vary according to the size of the firm.

Current Employment

Financial managers held about eight hundred thousand jobs in 2001. Although these managers are found in virtually every industry, about one-third are employed in the financial services industry—banks, finance companies, insurance companies, brokerage firms, and related institutions.

According to the U.S. Department of Labor, financial management is among the top forty occupations, with faster-than-average job growth projected. Skilled financial managers will become more sought-after with the increasing complexity of taxes and other financial matters and greater emphasis on accurate reporting of financial data. Most jobs will result from the need to replace those who transfer to other fields, retire, or leave the occupation for other reasons. Because of the increasing number of qualified applicants, competition is expected to increase. A broad base of familiarity with a range of financial management issues and with computers and data processing may enhance one's chances for employment. Expertise in a rapidly growing industry, such as health care, may also prove helpful.

Budget Analysts

The driving force behind all business planning is the allocation of limited resources: the budget. The budget determines how a company operates and whether it can expand or must marshal resources to weather an economic downturn. Budget analysis is an integral part of the decision-making process in most corporations and government agencies. Budget analysts play a primary role in the research, analysis, and development of budgets.

Nature of the Work

In small firms, the budget analyst is often an accountant or controller. Large firms may employ a whole retinue of analysts in a separate budget department overseen by the controller. In private industry, the analyst's job centers on seeking new ways to improve efficiency and increase profits. Government analysts, while (unfortunately) not concerned with profits, are also interested (we hope) in determining the most efficient distribution of funds and resources among various departments and programs. Analysts provide advice and technical assistance in preparing an organization's annual budget.

Analysts work with financial managers and department heads to prepare initial plans for expected programs, estimated costs, and necessary capital expenditures. Analysts then examine the budget estimates for completeness, accuracy, and conformance with the organization's objectives and procedures. They review financial requests by employing cost-benefit analysis, exploring alternative funding methods, and evaluating the requests in terms of the agency's priorities and financial resources.

After this review process, budget analysts consolidate the information into operating and financial budget summaries. Throughout the year, analysts periodically monitor the operating budget by reviewing reports and accounting records to determine if allocated funds have been expended as specified. They keep program managers and others within the organization informed on the status of their budgets and the availability of funds.

Training and Advancement

Most private firms and government agencies require candidates for the above listed job positions to have at least a bachelor's degree in business administration, accounting, finance, economics, or some closely related field. A growing number of employers prefer candidates with a master's degree, while some large corporations hire only certified public accountants. Since the budget process requires strong analytical skills, courses in mathematics, statistics, and computer science are highly recommended. The increasing computerization of the budget process in recent years suggests that this is an important area of study, especially in terms of the financial software packages available.

Entry-level professionals may receive some formal training when they begin their jobs, but most employers have new analysts work through one budget cycle as a member of a team. The federal government offers extensive on-the-job as well as classroom training for beginners. In many cases, the federal government will pay for advanced education.

Capable entry-level analysts can be promoted quickly into intermediate-level positions within the first two years and then into senior positions a few years later. Further promotion depends on skills and experience and involves added budgeting and supervisory responsibilities. In many cases, analysts capitalize on their close working relationships with top-level managers to advance into management positions. In addition, because financial and analytical skills are vital in any organization, analysts are often able to transfer to similar positions in other organizations.

Current Employment

Budget analysts held about 66,000 jobs throughout private industry and government in 2001. About one-third of all jobs were in federal, state, and local government offices. The Department of Defense has seven of every ten of those working for the federal government. The education services industry was the next largest employer, accounting for 8 percent of all jobs. Other major employers of budget analysts can include hospitals and manufacturers of transportation equipment, chemicals, and electrical and electronic machinery.

Job Outlook

Employment of budget analysts is expected to grow about as fast as the average for all occupations through the year 2005. Although demand is increasing, competition for budget analyst jobs should remain keen because of the increasing number of qualified applicants. The financial work performed by a budget analyst is an important function in every organization, regardless of prevailing economic conditions. Therefore, employment of budget analysts is generally not adversely affected during hard economic times when other workers may be laid off.

Financial Analysts

Budget analysts fall under the broader classification of financial analysts, who are most frequently employed in the budget or finance department of a company. Financial analysts are important to a variety of other departments, including planning, administration, manufacturing, and marketing.

The basic function of these analysts varies according to the department. An analyst in the marketing department would be involved not only with the marketing department's budget but with making projections of sales and revenue, taking into account prevailing economic conditions. The manufacturing department's financial analyst works with costs as well as demand for products, making financial projections with regard to return on investment and payback schedules. This analyst might also be responsible for preparing all the financial data to help management determine whether new products should be manufactured or when existing products should be eliminated.

Working conditions and salary levels are similar for all financial analysts, varying on the degree of education, experience, and responsibility. Earnings also vary from one industry to another and from one region to another. In general, large firms in large metropolitan areas tend to pay the highest salaries.

11

ACCOUNTING

THE ACCOUNTING PROFESSION is an old one with evidence in some form dating back to ancient Babylonia, about 3600 B.C. The first indication of modern bookkeeping dates from about 600 B.C., with business practices in ancient Rome.

There are several references to accounting practices in the Bible, particularly regarding budgeting. In the fifteenth century, a Franciscan monk named Luca Paciolo published a treatise on double-entry bookkeeping. Although Paciolo's work was the first truly significant work in the modern era on this subject, he wrote in his treatise that double-entry bookkeeping had been the basis of financial records of merchants and other businesspeople in the city-states of Italy for quite some time.

Accounting as a separate and important profession became evident in the British Isles during the nineteenth century. An organization of Scottish accountants, known as the Society of Accountants, was formed in Edinburgh in 1854. A similar society was formed one year later in Glasgow. During the next twenty-five years, several other accounting organizations began to spring up, first in cities all over England and Scotland and later in Wales.

These British accountants were primarily responsible for bringing accounting to the United States and developing it here. In 1887 the first organization of public accountants was formed in the United States. It was called the American Association of Public Accountants and eventually became known as the American Institute of Certified Public Accountants.

The accounting profession was elevated to new heights in America as a result of two important legislative events that occurred in the twentieth century—the income tax law of 1913 and the establishment of the Securities and Exchange Commission in 1933. Furthermore, as the federal and local governments began to tap corporations and individuals for income tax and the tax code became more complex, experts were required to analyze, assess, report, and advise people to help minimize their tax obligations. Accountants and auditors were needed for small businesses as well as large corporations and for middle- and lower-income households as well as for the wealthy.

Opportunities

In 1979 there were approximately 830,000 accountants and auditors in the United States. By 1988 this figure had grown by 16 percent to 963,000. For some time the total number of accountants and auditors stagnated with 962,000 in 1994. However, licensed certified public accountants, registered public accountants, and other accounting practitioners increased 50 percent from 320,000 in 1988 to more than 500,000 in 1994. The total number of financial record processors declined from 2,487,000 in 1983 to

2,197,000 in 1997, but increased slightly to 2,205,000 in 2001. There were 100,000 establishments in 2000, only slightly higher than the 99,000 counted in 1999.

There were 52,850 accountants and 90,270 bookkeepers working in financial institutions in 2001, compared to 49,870 accountants and 114,400 bookkeepers in 1999.

While the majority of employees were unlicensed management and government accountants and auditors, many had earned professional designations that are not state regulated. Most accountants and auditors work in metropolitan areas where accounting firms and central or regional offices of major business are concentrated. Ten percent of all accountants and auditors are self-employed, and this number is expected to grow.

Accountants and auditors are found in all kinds of business, industrial, and government organizations. Many work for service-oriented businesses, including retail stores of every kind, the entertainment business, and, most importantly, accounting and auditing firms. Manufacturing firms, the government, and wholesale and retail trade companies also employ accountants.

As you can see, working as an accountant is not restricted to working for an accounting firm. The possibilities for finding work in this field are enormous because sooner or later all companies and individuals need some type of accounting work.

Earnings

Salaries in accounting, as in most other professions, are a function of the level attained, training, work experience, and ability. In both public accounting and industry, salaries usually begin in the low twenties. Here the employer expects the applicant to have an undergraduate degree in accounting and an ability to communicate well.

In financial institutions, accountants' salaries range between $45,450 in depository institutions and $55,460 in securities firms. Bookkeepers average $30,252 in annual salaries.

Job Outlook

Accountants will continue to be in demand in the future because of the vital role they play in the management of businesses and government and because of the growing complexities of the taxation system in the United States. Employment in this field is expected to grow close to the average for all occupations until 2005.

Table 11.1 lists employment and salary information for accountants and bookkeepers.

Accounting Fields

Accountants prepare, analyze, and verify financial reports that furnish current financial data. There are basically four types of

Table 11.1 Financial Institutions Accountants and Bookkeepers Employed and Mean Annual Wage, 2001

Institution	Accountants		Bookkeepers	
	Employed	Mean Wage	Employed	Mean Wage
Depository Institutions	25,780	$45,450	63,820	$26,400
Nondepository Institutions	9,530	46,950	18,920	28,860
Securities/Commodities Dealers	13,070	55,460	14,370	36,410
Central Reserve	570	50,400	1,420	29,850
Mortgage Bankers	3,900	45,980	8,740	29,740
Total	52,850	48,848	90,270	30,252

Source: U.S. Department of Labor: bls.gov

accountants: public, management, government, and internal auditing. Accountants most often concentrate on one phase of accounting, such as auditing, preparing taxes, or setting up accounting systems. The following is a brief description of the four types of accountants.

Public Accounting

Public accountants help manage other people's money by offering accounting, tax, auditing, management, and advisory services. For businesses, in particular, public accountants set up and maintain accounting systems. They examine records, prepare budgets, and report on the company's financial condition.

Many public accountants are certified public accountants (C.P.A.s) who have passed licensing examinations. Other accountants who are not C.P.A.s may be licensed by the state in which they work. They have rights and duties like those of C.P.A.s and must follow the same code of ethics.

Public accountants also give individuals and families advice on money and tax matters. They prepare gift, estate, inheritance, and income tax statements. They work with lawyers and insurance and trust experts in developing and carrying out estate plans and in handling other money affairs. Public accountants who work for the government prepare financial reports, make sure facts are accurate, and gather financial data about federal, state, and/or local projects.

Management Accounting

Management accountants, who are also called industrial or private accountants, handle the financial records of their companies. Their job is to prepare financial reports to meet the public disclosure requirements of various stock exchanges, the Securities and

Exchange Commission, and other regulatory bodies. Nearly six out of every ten accountants are in this field. Management accountants can have a variety of titles within an organization, including cost accountant, financial analyst, tax specialist, treasurer, or comptroller.

Government Accounting

Government accountants work for federal, state, and local governments. They see that revenues are received and expenditures are made in accordance with laws and regulations. These accountants examine the records of government agencies and audit private businesses and individuals whose dealings are subject to government regulation. Government accountants can and do serve as investigators, bank examiners, and agents of the Internal Revenue Service.

Internal Auditing

Internal auditors examine and evaluate their firms' financial and information systems, management procedures, and internal controls to ensure that records are accurate and controls are adequate to protect against fraud and waste. They also review company operations, evaluating their efficiency, effectiveness, and compliance with corporate policies and procedures, laws, and government regulations.

Accounting Teachers

In addition to the fields outlined above, a small number of trained accountants staff the faculties of business and professional schools as accounting teachers, researchers, or administrators. Such professionals teach the principles and methods of their field to students.

They must have, in addition to an understanding of their field, teaching skills and an ability to write books and articles concerning their profession. Some accountants who are either self-employed or who work for a company might teach on a part-time basis. Besides teaching accounting, these accounting teachers also teach logic, mathematics, finance, marketing, management, behavioral sciences, and economics. They show students how to use their reasoning powers and how best to relate accounting to other practical applications of these subject areas.

Accounting Specialists

Accountants usually concentrate on one particular phase of the field. The following are some of the most common accounting specialties.

Tax Accountants

These accountants concentrate on matters of taxation, such as preparing income tax forms as well as giving clients advice on the pros and cons of new and existing changes in the tax law. After they examine accounts, they follow government regulations in figuring clients' taxes. Tax accountants offer tax-planning services and inform their clients about the effects of personal and business activities on taxes. They figure taxes, plan and set up tax record systems, and inform clients of dates on which taxes are due.

Internal Auditors

Auditors who verify the accuracy of a firm's financial records are called internal auditors. They look for waste or fraud. Internal auditing is a rapidly growing segment of the accounting field because today many firms make decisions based on financial reports instead of merely relying upon hearsay or subjective factors such as personal observation.

Budget Accountants

These accountants establish and maintain budgets. By doing so, they help managers make plans that match amounts of money they have to spend. They gather facts and present plans to executives who obtain and set aside funds for different company expenses. Budget accountants measure performance and report plan changes so that those working to reach company goals can take proper action.

Systems Analyst Accountants

Accountants who suggest changes in accounting systems that will give management more useful data with which to make decisions are called systems analyst accountants.

Cost Accountants

These accountants set up or control systems to determine costs of company products or other products so that they can tell management where the company's money is being spent. They use their knowledge of accounting and economics to analyze costs of production, distribution, and services.

The Accounting Profession

Regardless of the accountants' area of specialty, they share many of the same characteristics, whether employed by an accounting firm or in the accounting department of a major corporation. The basic skills needed to become an accountant and the widespread need for accountants in all industries enable the accounting professional to transfer readily from one field to another. Once an accountant specializes in a particular industry or type of accounting, he or she becomes especially valuable within that field.

Working Conditions

Most accountants work in offices and generally keep regular hours. An exception may be those who are self-employed and might work out of their homes or set up their own hours. The traditional time for the preparation of income tax returns usually requires tax accountants.

Training and Advancement

The majority of accounting firms and those businesses that employ accountants usually require their accountants to have at least a bachelor's degree in accounting. Familiarity with computers and database software is also extremely important and, of course, there are accounting positions that require a master's degree or C.P.A. For starting accounting and auditing positions with the U.S. federal government, four years of college are required. This four-year degree must include at least twenty-four semester hours in accounting or auditing.

Accounting is offered as a major study in many universities across the country. Colleges accredited by the American Assembly of Collegiate Schools of Business (nacsb.edu) meet standards of business administration programs that include accounting. Junior and community colleges also offer courses and programs in accounting.

Many colleges offer students opportunities for experience with summer jobs, internship programs, or the financial management of campus organizations. Such experience is invaluable when it comes to landing that first full-time job.

Professional Certification

In addition to education and work experience, another important avenue for career advancement is through professional certification. Anyone who is a C.P.A. must have a certificate and a license issued by a state board of accountancy. All states use the Uniform C.P.A. Examination, which is prepared by the American Institute of Certified Public Accountants. This examination is divided into four separate parts, and the examinee is not required to pass all of them at one time. Most states require candidates to pass at least two parts almost immediately for partial credit and the balance within a certain time limit.

The vast majority of states require that C.P.A. candidates have a college degree, but a few specify that work experience may be substituted. Most states want candidates to have had some public accounting work experience.

Based on recommendations made by the American Institute of Certified Public Accountants and the National Association of State Boards of Accountancy, nine states presently require and twenty-five more will very soon require that C.P.A. candidates complete 150 semester hours of college education with a major in accounting. This 150-hour rule requires an additional year of college education beyond the usual four-year bachelor's degree in accounting. This requirement may become more common in the coming years. Obviously, the more education and work experience, the better chance one has of advancing.

Licensing

Licensure is also a requirement in several states. In the majority of states, C.P.A.s are the only accountants who are licensed and regulated. To work as a C.P.A. you must have a certificate as well as a license, or permit, issued by the state board of accountancy. The designation public accountant (P.A.) or registered public accountant (R.P.A.) is also recognized by thirty-eight states. However, with the dramatic growth in the number of C.P.A.s, most states are phasing out the P.A. or R.P.A. designation. Qualifications for those licensed as a P.A. or R.P.A. are less stringent, in some cases requiring only a high school diploma.

Professional Societies

Societies such as the Institute of Internal Auditors or the National Association of Accountants confer certification that attests to professional competence in a specialized field of accounting and auditing. This skill may be a result of work experience and examination or it may be the culmination of a series of training programs and examinations.

Certified Internal Auditors

Certified internal auditors must have completed two years of work experience in internal auditing and have successfully passed an examination prepared by the Institute of Internal Auditors, Incorporated. The institute has the authority to confer upon all applicants a certification. The National Association of Accountants (NAA) gives the Certificate in Management Accounting (CMA) to those who pass a series of exams and meet specific academic requirements.

The Accreditation Council for Accountancy

A division of the National Society of Public Accountants, the Accreditation Council for Accountancy awards a Certificate of Accreditation in Accountancy and a Certificate of Accreditation in Taxation to those who have passed comprehensive examinations. Prospective accountants must have an aptitude for mathematics; be able to analyze, compare, and interpret facts and figures quickly; and make sound judgments based on their specific knowledge. Accuracy and the ability to handle responsibility with limited supervision are also important.

Beginning public accountants usually start by assisting with auditing work, advancing to intermediate positions with more responsibility within two years, then to senior positions within another few years. Beginning management accountants often start as ledger accountants, junior internal auditors, or as trainees for technical accounting positions. They may eventually advance to such positions as chief plant accountant, chief cost accountant, budget director, or manager of internal auditing, controller, treasurer, financial vice president, or chief financial officer.

The American Accounting Association promotes worldwide excellence in accounting education, research, and practice. Founded in 1916 as the American Association of University Instructors in Accounting, its present name was adopted in 1936. The association is a voluntary organization of persons interested in accounting education and research.

Appendix A

Financial Associations and Employers

For more information contact the following associations, organizations, and major employers in banking, the securities industry, financial services, insurance and real estate, and accounting.

Banking Associations and Organizations

American Bankers Association
1120 Connecticut Ave. NW
Washington, DC 20036
aba.com

American Institute of Banking
19923 S. Plantation Estate Dr.
Porter, TX 77365
aba.com/conferences+and+education/aib_main.htm

Bank Administration Institute (BAI)
1 N. Franklin, Ste. 1000
Chicago, IL 60606-3421
bai.org

Bureau of Public Debt
Consumers Service and Current Income Branch
Parkersburg, WV 26106-2186
publicdebt.treas.gov

Consumer Bankers Association
1000 Wilson Blvd.
Arlington, VA 22209-2500
cbanet.org

Credit Union National Association
P.O. Box 431
Madison, WI 53701-0431
cuna.org

Federal Deposit Insurance Corporation
550 Seventeenth St. NW
Washington, DC 20429
fdic.gov

Federal Financial Institutions Examination Council (FFIEC)
2100 Pennsylvania Ave. NW
Washington, DC 30037
ffiec.gov

Federal Reserve System
Board of Governors
Twentieth St. and Constitution Ave. NW
Washington, DC 20551
federalreserve.gov

Federal Trade Commission (FTC)
600 Pennsylvania Ave. NW
Washington, DC 20580
ftc.gov

The Institute of Financial Education
111 E. Wacker Dr.
Chicago, IL 60601
financial-education-icfe.org

Mortgage Bankers Association
1919 Pennsylvania Ave. NW
Washington, DC 20006-3438
mbaa.org

National Council of Savings Institutions
1101 Fifteenth St. NW
Washington, DC 20005
bankmag.com

National Credit Union Administration (NCUA)
1775 Duke St.
Alexandria, VA 22314
ncua.gov

National Technical Information Service (NTIS)
5285 Port Royal Rd.
Springfield, VA 22151
ntis.gov/fcpc

Office of the Comptroller of the Currency (OCC)
1301 McKinney St., Ste. 3710
Houston, TX 77010
occ.treas.gov

Major Employers in Banking

Bank of Boston
Boston, MA
bos.frb.org

BankAmerica Corp.
San Francisco, CA
bankofamerica.com

Bankers Trust New York Corp.
New York, NY
bankertrust.com

Citibank
New York, NY
citibank.com

First Union Corporation
Charlotte, NC
firstunion.com

First Wachovia Corp.
Winston-Salem, NC
wachovia.com

J. P. MorganChase
New York, NY
jpmorganchase.com

Mellon Bank Corp.
Pittsburgh, PA
mellon.com

Norwest Corp.
Minneapolis, MN
norwestcorp.com

U.S. Bancorp (USB)
Minneapolis, MN
usbank.com

Securities Industry Associations and Organizations

American Stock Exchange
86 Trinity Pl.
New York, NY 10006
amex.com

Certified Financial Planner
Board of Standards
1700 Broadway, Ste. 2100
Denver, CO 80290
cfp.net

Chicago Board Options Exchange
400 S. LaSalle St.
Chicago, IL 60605
cboe.com/home/default.asp

Financial Planning Association
Two Concourse Pkwy., Ste. 800
Atlanta, GA 30328
fpanet.org

National Association of Personal Financial Advisors
3250 N. Arlington Heights Rd., Ste. 101
Arlington Heights, IL 60004
npfa.org

National Association of Securities Dealers
1735 K St. NW
Washington, DC 20006
nasd.com

New York Stock Exchange
111 Wall St.
New York, NY 10005
nysedata.com

Pacific Stock Exchange
301 Pine St.
San Francisco, CA 94104
pacificex.com

Securities and Exchange Commission (SEC)
450 Fifth St. NW
Washington, DC 20549
sec.gov

Securities Industry Association
120 Broadway
New York, NY 10271-0080
sia.com

Security Traders Association
420 Lexington Ave, Ste. 2334
New York, NY 10170
securitytraders.org

Major Employers in the Securities Industry

Bear Stearns and Company
New York, NY
bearstearns.com

Credit Suisse First Boston
New York, NY
csfb.com

Dain, Bosworth, Inc.
Minneapolis, MN

Dain Rauscher, Inc.
Dallas, TX
rbcdain.com

Lazard Frères and Company
New York, NY
lazard.com

Merrill Lynch Pierce Fenner and Smith, Inc.
New York, NY
ml.com

Morgan Stanley and Company
New York, NY
morganstanley.com
morganstanley.com/careers/index.html

Paine Webber
New York, NY
painewebber.com

Smith Barney, Harris Upham and Company, Inc.
New York, NY
smithbarney.com

Financial Services Associations and Organizations

American Financial Services Association
1101 Fourteenth St. NW, 4th Fl.
Washington, DC 20005
americanfinsvcs.com

Association for Financial Professionals
http://afponline.jobcontrolcenter.com/apply/profile.cfm

Financial Analysts Federation
Boar's Head La., No. 5
P.O. Box 3726
Charlottesville, VA 22903
effas.com

Financial Executives Institute
10 Madison Ave.
P.O. Box 1938
Morristown, New Jersey 07960
fei.org

Financial Management Association International
    (student organization)
School of Business
University of South Florida
Tampa, FL 33620
fma.org

Financial Managers Society
111 E. Wacker Dr.
Chicago, IL 60601
fmsinc.org

Financial Planning Association
1615 L St. NW, Ste. 650
Washington, DC 20036
fpanet.org

Healthcare Financial Management Association, HFMA
2 Westbrook Corporate Center, Ste. 700
Westchester, IL 60154
hfma.org

Insurance and Real Estate Associations and Organizations

Institute of Real Estate Management
430 N. Michigan Ave.
Chicago, IL 60611-4090
irem.org

National Association of Home Builders
1201 Fifteenth St., NW
Washington, DC 20005
nahb.org

National Association of Professional Insurance Agents
400 N. Washington St.
Alexandria, VA 22314
pianet.com

National Association of Realtors
30700 Russell Ranch Rd.
Westlake Village, CA 91362
realtor.com

Accounting Associations and Organizations

Accountants for the Public Interest
1625 I St. NW, Ste. 717
Washington, DC 20006
geocities.com/api_woods/api/apihome.html

Accreditation Council for Accountancy and Taxation, Inc.
1010 N. Fairfax St.
Alexandria, VA 22314-1574
acatcredential.org

American Accounting Association
5717 Bessie Dr.
Sarasota, FL 33423
http://aaahq.org

American Institute of Certified Public Accountants
1211 Avenue of the Americas
New York, NY 10036
aicpa.org

American Society of Tax Professionals
P.O. Box 1027
Sioux Falls, SD 57101
taxsites.com

American Society of Women Accountants
35 E. Wacker Dr.
Chicago, IL 60601
aswa.org

Association of Government Accountants
2208 Vermont Ave.
Alexandria, VA 22301
agacgfm.org

Financial Executives Institute
10 Madison Ave.
P.O. Box 1938
Morristown, NJ 07960
fei.org

Institute of Management Accounting
215 City Center Bldg.
Ann Arbor, MI 48104
ioma.com

National Association of Black Accountants
1642 R St. NW
Washington, DC 20009
nabainc.org

Colleges and Universities Offering Majors in Banking and Finance

Arizona

University of Arizona
Robert L. Nugent Bldg.
Tucson, AZ 85721
arizona.edu

California

California State University
5151 State University Dr.
Los Angeles, CA 90032
calstatela.edu

Santa Clara University
500 El Camino Real
Santa Clara, CA 95053
scu.edu

Colorado

Colorado State University
Fort Collins, CO 80523-0015
colostate.edu

Connecticut

Fairfield University
1073 N. Benson Rd.
Fairfield, CT 06430
fairfield.edu

University of Connecticut
2131 Hillside Rd., Unit 3088
Storrs, CT 06269
uconn.edu

Florida

Florida International University
University Park Campus, PC 140
Miami, FL 33199
flu.edu

Florida State University
A2500 University Center
Tallahassee, FL 32306
fsu.edu

University of Central Florida
Box 160111
Orlando, FL 32816
ucf.edu

University of Miami
1252 Memorial Dr.
Coral Gables, FL 33124
miami.edu

Georgia

University of Georgia
212 Terrell Hall
Athens, GA 30602
uga.edu

Illinois

DePaul University
1 E. Jackson Blvd.
Chicago, IL 60604
depaul.edu

Loyola University of Chicago
820 N. Michigan Ave.
Chicago, IL 60611
luc.edu

North Central College
P.O. Box 3065
Naperville, IL 60566
noctri.edu

Quincy University
1800 College Ave.
Quincy, IL 62301
quincy.edu

Indiana

Butler University
4600 Sunset Ave.
Indianapolis, IN 46208
butler.edu

Purdue University, Calumet
171 St. and Wodmart Ave.
Hammond, IN 46323
calumet.edu

University of Evansville
1800 Lincoln Dr.
Evansville, IN 47722
evansville.edu

University of Notre Dame
220 Main Bldg.
South Bend, IN 46556
nd.edu

Valparaiso University
651 S. College Ave.
Valparaiso, IN 46383
valpo.edu

Iowa

Drake University
2507 University Ave.
Des Moines, IA 50311
drake.edu

University of Dubuque
2000 University Ave.
Dubuque, IA 52001
dbq.edu

University of Iowa
107 Calvin Hall
Iowa City, IA 52242
uiowa.edu

Wartburg College
100 Wartburg Blvd.
Waverly, IA 50677
wartburg.edu

Kentucky

Murray State University
1 Murray St.
Murray, KY 42071
murraystate.edu

Louisiana

Loyola University New Orleans
6363 St. Charles Ave.
New Orleans, LA 70118
loyno.edu

Maryland

University of Maryland
Mitchell Bldg.
College Park, MD 20742
maryland.edu

Massachusetts

Babson College
Mustard Hall
Babson Park, MA 02457
babson.edu

Bentley College
175 Forest St.
Waltham, MA 02452-4705
bentley.edu

Boston College
140 Commonwealth Ave.
Chestnut Hill, MA 02467
bc.edu

Michigan

Grand Valley State University
1 Campus Dr.
Allendale, MI 49401
gvsu.edu

Hillsdale College
33 E. College St.
Hillsdale, MI 49242
hillsdale.edu

Minnesota

Winona State University
Office of Admissions
Winona, MN 55987
winona.edu

Mississippi

Mississippi State University
Box 6305
Mississippi State, MS 39762
msstate.edu

Nebraska

Creighton University
2500 California Plaza
Omaha, NE 68178
creighton.edu

New Jersey

Richard Stockton College
Jim Leds Rd.
Pomona, NJ 08240
stockton.edu

Rutgers University
406 Penn St.
Camden, NJ 08102
rutgers.edu

New York

Clarkson University
Holcroft House
P.O. Box 5605
Potsdam, NY 13699-5605
clarkson.edu

Fordham University
441 E. Fordham Rd.
Bronx, NY 10458
fordham.edu

New York University
22 Washington Sq. North
New York, NY 10011
nyu.edu

Rochester Institute of Technology
60 Lomb Memorial Dr.
Rochester, NY 14623
rit.edu

Siena College
515 Loudon Rd.
Loudonville, NY 12211
siena.edu

North Carolina

Wake Forest University
P.O. Box 7305, Reynolds Station
Winston-Salem, NC 27109
wfu.edu

Ohio

Cedarville University
251 N. Main St.
Cedarville, OH 45314
cedarville.edu

Ohio Northern University
525 S. Main St.
Ada, OH 45801
onu.edu

Oklahoma

University of Oklahoma
1000 Asp Ave.
Norman, OK 73019
ou.edu

Oregon

Linfield College
900 SE Baker St.
McMinnville, OR 97128
linfield.edu

Pennsylvania

Chestnut Hill College
Pittsburgh, PA 19118
chc.edu

Duquesne University
600 Forbes Ave.
Pittsburgh, PA 15282
duq.edu

Juniata College
Eighteenth and Moore Sts.
Huntington, PA 16652
juniata.edu

Penn State University
201 Shields Bldg.
Penn State University Park, PA 16804
psu.edu

St. Joseph's University
5600 City Ave.
Philadelphia, PA 19131
sju.edu

University of Pennsylvania
One College Hall
Philadelphia, PA 19104
upenn.edu

Rhode Island

Providence College
549 River Ave.
Providence, RI 02198
providence.edu

South Carolina

Wofford College
429 N. Church St.
Spartanburg, SC 29303
wofford.edu

Tennessee

Lincoln Memorial University
Cumberland Gap Pkwy.
Harrogate, TN 37752
lmunet.edu

Union University
1050 Union University Dr.
Jackson, TN 38305
uu.edu

University of Memphis
229 Administration Bldg.
Memphis, TN 38152
memphis.edu

University of Tennessee
131 Hooper Hall
Chattanooga, TN 37403
utc.edu

Texas

Baylor University
Waco, TX 76798
baylor.edu

Southern Methodist University
Box 750296
Dallas, TX 75275
smu.edu

Texas Christian University
TCU Box 297013
Fort Worth, TX 76129
tcu.edu

University of Saint Thomas
3800 Montrose Blvd.
Houston, TX 77006
stthom.edu

Utah

University of Utah
201 S. 1460 E, Rm. 250S
Salt Lake City, UT 84112
utah.edu

Virginia

James Madison University
Sonner Hall MSC 0101
Harrisonburg, VA 22807
jmu.edu

Washington

University of Washington
Box 355840
Seattle, WA 98195
washington.edu

Washington, D.C.

American University
4400 Massachusetts Ave. NW
Washington, DC 20016
american.edu

Wisconsin

Marquette University
P.O. Box 1881
Milwaukee, WI 53201
marquette.edu

RECOMMENDED READING

THE FOLLOWING RESOURCES will give you a lot of information about the various sectors that make up the financial services occupations.

Banking Resources

Books and Pamphlets

American Bank Directory. Norcross, Ga.: McFadden Business Publications, continually updated.

Chernow, Ron. *The House of Morgan: An American Banking Dynasty and the Rise of Modern Finance.* Berkeley: Publishers Group West, 2001.

Evans, Joel R. *Careers in Financial Services.* Hempstead, N.Y.: Hofstra University, School of Business Press, 1996.

Houpt, James V. *International Trends for U.S. Banks and Banking Markets.* Staff Study, Board of Governors of the Federal Reserve System, May 1988.

Logue, Dennis E., ed. *Handbook of Modern Finance*. Boston: Warren, Gorham, and Lamont, Inc., 1994.

Mainstream Access, Inc. *The Banking Job Finder*. Englewood Cliffs, N.J.: Prentice-Hall, 1981.

Paradis, Adrian, A. Phillips, and A. Perry. *Opportunities in Banking Careers*. Chicago: VGM Career Books, 2000.

Rosenberg, Jerry M. *Dictionary of Banking and Financial Services*. New York: John Wiley and Sons, 1985.

———. *Dictionary of Banking*. New York: John Wiley and Sons, 1993.

Simpson, Carolyn. *Choosing a Career in Banking and Finance*. New York: Rosen Publications Group, 1999.

U.S. Department of Commerce, Bureau of Industrial Economics. "Commercial Banking," in *U.S. Industrial Outlook*. Washington, D.C.: G.P.O.

U.S. Department of Labor, Bureau of Labor Statistics. *Occupational Outlook Handbook*. Washington, D.C.: G.P.O., biennial.

Periodicals

ABA Bankers Weekly, aba.com

American Banker (monthly), americanbanker.com

American Banker ONLINE, americanbanker.com

The Bankers Magazine (monthly), Warren, Gorham, and Lamont, Inc., 210 South St., Boston, MA 02111

Bankers Monthly, aba.com

Independent Community Bankers of America, iba.org /index-main.html

Journal of Commercial Bank Lending (monthly), Robert Morris
    Associates, 1 Liberty Pl., Ste. 2300, 1650 Market St.,
    Philadelphia, PA 19103
Trust Management Update (monthly), aba.com

Securities Industry Resources

Books

Gourgues, Harold W., Jr. *Financial Planning Handbook.*
    New York: New York Institute of Finance, 1983.
Hallman, Victor G., and Jerry Rosenbloom. *Personal Financial
    Planning.* New York: McGraw-Hill, 2000.
Hurley, Gale E., and Cynthia G. Hurley. *Personal Money
    Management: A Consumer Guide.* Upper Saddle River, N.J.:
    Prentice Hall, 1976.
Madura, Jeff. *Financial Markets and Institutions,* 2000.
Mishkin, Frederick S. *Reading Money, Banking, and Financial
    Institutions.* New York: Addison-Wesley, 1988.
Securities and Exchange Commission. *Broker-Dealer Directory.*
    Washington, D.C.: annual.
Security Dealers of North America. New York: Standard and Poor's,
    semiannual.
Who's Who in the Securities Industry. Chicago: Economist
    Publishing Company, 2000.

Periodicals

The Banker, thebanker.com
Barron's (weekly), barrons.com
Business Week (weekly), businessweek.com

CNBC.com

CNN/Money, http://money.cnn.com

Dallas Business Journal, http://dallas.bizjournal.com

Dun's Business Month (monthly), Dun and Bradstreet Corp., 875 Third Ave., New York, NY 10022

The Economist, economist.com

Financial Planning News (monthly), International Association for Financial Planning, 2 Concourse Pkwy., Atlanta, GA 30328

Financial World (bimonthly), Macro Communications, Inc., 1250 Broadway, New York, NY 10001

Forbes (biweekly), forbes.com

Fortune (biweekly), fortuneeducation.com

Investment Dealers Digest (weekly), iddmagazine.com

Kiplinger Online, kiplinger.com

Money (monthly), http://money.cnn.com

Personal Finance, http://money central/msn.com

Securities Industry Trends (monthly), sia.com/publications

The Wall Street Journal, http://online.wsj.com

Weekly Bond Buyer (weekly), 1 State Street Plaza, New York, NY 10004

Financial Services Resources

Periodicals

Business Credit (monthly), http://library.nesu.edu

Financial Analysts Journal (bimonthly), aimr.com/publications/faj

Financial Executive (bimonthly), fei.org/magazine/current.cfm

Financial Management (monthly), fma.org
Financial Management Service: A Bureau of the U.S.
    Department of the Treasury, http://fms.treas.gov
Financial World (monthly), financialworld.co.uk
Investment Management News:
    CNN Money, cnnfn.com
    MSN Money, moneycentrl.msn.com
    NASDAQ, nasdaq.com
    New York Stock Exchange, nyse.com
Journal of Cost Analysis (semiannual),
    sceaonline.net/publications/journ_main.htm
Journal of Financial and Quantitative Analysis, University of
    Washington, Seattle, http://depts.washington.edu/jfqa
*Journal of International Financial Management and
    Accounting*, blackwellpublishing.com

Insurance and Real Estate Resources

Books

Baldwin, Ben. *New Life Insurance Investment Advisor*. New York:
    McGraw-Hill Companies, 2001.
Kennedy, Danielle. *Double Your Income in Real Estate*. Franklin
    Lakes, N.J.: Career Press, 1998.
Rejnis, Ruth. *The Everything Homebuying Book: How to List and
    Sell Real Estate in the 21st Century*. Holbrook, Mass.: Adams
    Media Corp., 1998.
Roberts, Ralph. *Sell It Yourself*. Holbrook, Mass.: Adams Media
    Corp., 1999.
Schrayer, Robert M. *Opportunities in Insurance Careers*.
    Lincolnwood: VGM Career Books, 1999.

Sumichrast, Michael, and Ronald G. Shafer. *The New Complete Book of Home Buying*. New York: Dow Jones-Irwin, 1990.

Accounting Resources

Books

Davidson, Sidney, and Clyde P. Stickney. *How to Speak Accounting: A Glossary of Terms with Guidance on How to Read an Annual Report*. New York: Harcourt Brace Jovanovich, 1983.

Stevens, Mark. *The Big Six*. New York: Simon and Schuster, 1991.

Periodicals

CPA Journal (monthly), cpajournal.com

Government Accountants Journal (quarterly), Association of Government Accountants, 727 S. Twenty-Third St., Arlington, VA 22202

Journal of Accountancy (monthly), findarticles.com

Management Accounting (monthly), National Association of Accountants, 10 Paragon Dr., Montvale, NJ 07645

The Practical Accountant (monthly), luhman.org

About the Authors

MICHAEL SUMICHRAST, NOW retired, was the chairman of the board of Eastbrokers International, Inc. Prior to joining Eastbrokers, Sumichrast was a chief economist and senior staff vice president of the National Association of Home Builders. He has built more than three thousand housing units and commercial and industrial buildings in Australia and the United States and has served as a consulting engineer in Asia and Latin America.

Dr. Sumichrast studied industrial engineering in Czechoslovakia, continued his studies at Melbourne University in Australia, and received his M.B.A. and Ph.D. in economics from Ohio State University. For six years he was a professor at American University.

Sumichrast wrote a weekly column for the *Washington Post* and housing-oriented articles for the *Washington Star*. He has also authored several books, which have been published by Dow Jones–Irwin, Universal Publishing, and Dow Jones Books. Dr. Sumichrast's books include *Planning Your Retirement Housing* (Scott, Foresman and Company for the American Association of Retired Persons), *Where Will You Live Tomorrow?* (Dow Jones–Irwin), *The*

Complete Book of Home Buying (Bantam Books, paperback), and *The New Complete Book of Home Buying* (Dow Jones–Irwin, hardback). Other publications include *Housing Markets* (Dow Jones–Irwin), *Opportunities in Building Construction Trades* (VGM Career Books), and numerous other books, papers, and articles. This is the fourth edition of *Opportunities in Financial Careers*.

Dr. Sumichrast's new book, *Rebirth of Freedom: From Nazis and Communists to a New Life in America*, was first published in Slovak in Bratislava in 1996 and in 1999 by Hellgate Press in the United States, with a foreword by General Alexander M. Haig, Jr.

Martin A. Sumichrast is a born entrepreneur and business builder. In 1980, as a junior in college, he began working with his father, Dr. Michael Sumichrast—with whom he coauthored *Opportunities in Financial Careers*—in real estate development. In the late 1990s, Martin Sumichrast's career turned to investment banking and the securities business. In 1993, at the age of twenty-six, Mr. Sumichrast started his first publicly traded company, Global Capital Partners, which he grew into a multinational, full-service investment banking firm and which in early 2000 employed more than three hundred people in nine countries and managed over $1 billion in more than forty thousand customer accounts. Mr. Sumichrast has also served on various boards of private and public companies. Mr. Sumichrast now manages a private venture capital and business advisory firm, Lomond International, Inc., based in Charlotte, North Carolina.

Martin Sumichrast is coauthor with Michael Sumichrast and Ronald G. Shafer of an upcoming book, *The Complete Book of Home Buying for Today's Consumers.*